BETTER MAKE IT REAL

BETTER MAKE IT REAL

Creating Authenticity in an Increasingly Fake World

Jill J. Morin

Mark —
Keep it real!

PRAEGER

AN IMPRINT OF ABC-CLIO, LLC
Santa Barbara, California • Denver, Colorado • Oxford, England

Copyright 2010 by Jill J. Morin

**Library of Congress Cataloging-in-Publication Data is available at
www.loc.gov**

ISBN: 978-0-313-37680-1
EISBN: 978-0-313-37681-8

14 13 12 11 10   2 3 4 5

This book is also available on the World Wide Web as an eBook.
Visit www.abc-clio.com for details.

Praeger
An Imprint of ABC-CLIO, LLC

ABC-CLIO, LLC
130 Cremona Drive, P.O. Box 1911
Santa Barbara, California 93116-1911

This book is printed on acid-free paper ∞
Manufactured in the United States of America

To my friends and colleagues at
Kahler Slater, whose passion, dedication,
and talent inspire me each and every day.

CONTENTS

ACKNOWLEDGMENTS

This book has been in the making for many years. It began with the notion that someone should document the ideas and innovations our firm, Kahler Slater®, was in the process of discovering as we started down the path of our own organizational transformation. As the only person in the firm with a journalism degree among a group of mostly architects at the time, I became the most likely "volunteer" to become the author. But it wasn't until, after mostly talking about this book for ten years, a Kahler Slater colleague of mine at the time, who had pestered me for years with numerous emails as well as lunchtime and cocktail chats about the project, sent me an email titled "The Challenge." In this most beautiful of messages, the sender quoted William James and John Milton in his plea to get me to stop talking and start writing. Thank you, Joe. I finally took your advice.

A perhaps less eloquent, but nonetheless effective, verbal shove came from author Peter Block, who asked me, in his typically direct way, "What in the hell are you waiting for? Write the book!" Thanks to Peter, and to my first editor, Judy Bridges of Redbird Studio, the first draft of this book was completed in a year, in between my day job at Kahler Slater and my even more important job as a wife and mother. My husband, Kent, and my two children, Kelsey and Nicholas, spent many hours tiptoeing around the house while I wrote, offering me a calm oasis as well as unending and unconditional support. For this and for so much more, I can never thank them enough.

So many people contributed to this effort—reading draft chapters, helping me to organize my thoughts, giving me a push when I needed one, conducting research, and simply listening to me whine about how much harder it is to write a book than I ever thought it would be. So, special thanks go to Kimberly Rosby (executive assistant extraordinaire), Kelly Gaglione, Kurt Thieding, Dean Amhaus, Robert Deahl, Lyn Geboy, Rich Teerlink, Chic Thompson, Felicity Librie, Gretchen Pfaehler, Jeff Neidorfler, Carla Minsky, Mike Brown, Pat Foran, Nicole Fermanian, Karen Vernal, Wendy Heintz-Joehnk, Janet Slater, and Mary Louise Dean.

I began my own personal transformational journey to become an author with much professional help. Thanks to Jeff Olson, my supremely patient and wise editor. Writers Richard Fraser and Carolyn Washburne, in particular, were there for me, and more recently, Martha Finney, my journalistic Sherpa, was and is a constant source of guidance. Thank you, Martha, for taking this neophyte under your experienced wings. I could never have come this far without you.

Thanks to all of our clients who entrust us with their hopes and dreams. And thanks especially to those who were so gracious to allow us to share their stories in this book.

And finally, it's obvious that this book would not have come to be had it not been for the people, past and present, who are Kahler Slater. From David Kahler and Mac Slater, who had the vision and tenacity to guide and grow a small midwestern architecture firm toward a bigger playing field, to my fellow executive officers, George Meyer and Jim Rasche, who picked up the slack at the office while I was at home, pounding the keyboard. This book simply would not have happened without the insight, support, and leadership of George and Jim. Thanks guys.

And thanks to all of the staff at Kahler Slater. This book seeks to capture and illuminate the magic that you work, day in and day out, guiding clients toward their authentic transformations, and designing total experiences that make them manifest. Your work is transforming the design profession about which you all care so deeply, as you seek to enhance life through artful design. I hope that providing readers with this brief glimpse into your world continues to inspire you and the clients whom you serve, now and in the future.

INTRODUCTION

The words printed here are concepts. You must go through the experiences.

Saint Augustine

Most choices in life usually present us with the chance for a do-over. A car purchase, for instance. You'll most likely do that more than once. Don't like the coffee or service you got at yesterday's café? Go to a different one today. Are your instincts flashing Code Red in the back of your mind while talking with a potential business partner, employer, or employee? Cut the conversation short and usher that person out the door. Sure, there's a disappointment, but that's nothing compared with the worry, loss of energy and money, and unrecoverable waste of time that a star-crossed commitment would have represented.

Other choices in life don't leave much room for reconsideration. Marriage, for instance, is at least *supposed* to be a one-time only event. Consequently, one's 25th wedding anniversary is probably going to happen only once in a person's life. Another choice that really can't be changed in, shall we say, midstream, is a luxury cruise. When you're long into a cruise and you realize you've made a big mistake, chances are you're stuck with that decision, at least until you reach the next port—or you have the kind of budget that can easily absorb a rescue helicopter.

So, when you combine the two—25th anniversary and luxury cruise—you're a customer with high expectations and much at stake. There's a lot invested in your choice. So naturally, everything has to be perfect down to the last detail.

When my husband, Kent, and I started thinking of ways to celebrate our 25th anniversary, we decided on that luxury cruise—but with some trepidation. What if we put our money down, got into the middle of the ocean, only to discover that we wanted nothing more than to get the heck off *right now?* But we followed a trusted friend's advice and selected SeaDream Yacht Club for our big event. And everything was just as it was advertised—and reputed—to be. The personal and customized service, the champagne and caviar reception, the fresh flowers and the Belgian linens, food that looked like a Renaissance still-life painting and tasted divine, everything perfect down to the last, most minute detail.

Until the first night. Around 2:00 A.M., Kent and I woke up to the sound of alarms, bells, and whistles. It stopped pretty quickly, so we went back to sleep. The next morning a glance out the window told us we were still out to sea when we should have been portside in Valencia, the first stop on our itinerary. We found a note slipped under our door. It was from the captain, telling us that one of the engines had caught fire overnight. Nothing to worry about, really. We're just limping along on one engine, and the first order of business is to get that engine repaired—which meant that our itinerary was blown to smithereens. We would not be seeing the port of Ibiza. And we'd be waylaid in Valencia for a day or two while waiting for the repairs to be completed.

For those passengers counting on sticking to that particular itinerary, I'm sure it must have been a terrible disappointment to be forced to miss those ports of call. But I was plenty happy with what I could see from the deck, reclining on my *Balinese Dream Bed,* a cold beverage in hand. From my perspective as a CEO obsessed with how companies live out their brand proposition by the way they treat their customers and clients, I could see plenty as a luxuriating passenger watching the ship's values in action from the deck. (No matter how relaxing the vacation, the business hat really never does come off, does it?) And what I saw was more interesting than even the views of Valencia:

- The ship's engineers, who had been immediately flown to Spain from their station in Germany to work on the problem, which they did around the clock until the engine was fixed.
- The ship's director of entertainment, who hired local Flamenco dancers to entertain us, and set up a huge screen on deck, allowing for an impromptu outdoor rock concert video to be shown under the stars to prevent us from getting bored as we waited for the repairs to be completed.
- The ship's owner, who happened to be aboard the yacht during the trip, personally apologizing to all of his guests, and offering us complimentary massages in the ship's spa, a full rebate on the days we were stuck in port, as well as waiving all land excursion fees, and offering a generous discount on future bookings, which a number of the 100 guests took full advantage of before the cruise ended.

For cruises run by other companies, we on the mainland know that things have gone awry by watching disgruntled (or sick or scared) passengers talking into cameras on CNN, swearing they'll never sail again. And on this cruise, there were disappointments, to be sure. But the net result of those unplanned scenarios was that more passengers signed up for additional cruises before leaving the ship than is typical for the cruise line. And Kent and I said to each other: "If we ever go on another cruise, we will only go on a SeaDream Yacht Club cruise."

Pay attention to how we worded this agreement: not only would we use SeaDream Yacht Club again, we would *only* use SeaDream Yacht Club—*to the exclusion of all other lines in the luxury cruise space.* This is one do-over we'd happily do over again, exactly the same way.

The reason: because of the way in which this cruise line extended its value promise to its clients and then lived out that value proposition, regardless of unexpected circumstances, it has made itself a company that is so integrally self-possessed in what it does, stands for, offers to its clients, and treats its own people, it doesn't have to compete with its competitors. At least in the opinion of these two customers.

Any cruise line can serve up a chilled lobster salad on deck, and keep the drinks cold and coming. But what the SeaDream Yacht Club did to secure our loyalty to the company was the authentic experience it provided: the way it walked its talk. Sure, we shared their frustration in their inability to get us back out to sea as quickly as we had all hoped. The engine part that was needed to get us going again was not readily available. And the generator they rented from a local source stopped working in the middle of the night, leading to temperatures hovering around 80 uncomfortable degrees in the cabins. So, they made up extra beds on deck (those Balinese beds really came in handy!) as well as in the much-cooler library. And they did so with such genuine care, concern, and good humor that the whole thing ended up feeling like a group slumber party.

Stuff happens, and it happens to even the best of companies. The way in which the SeaDream staff handled this particular stuff actually provided an opportunity for them to shine in the face of adversity. They passed this particular test with flying colors, which resulted in increased customer admiration and loyalty, despite the mishaps and flaws of this particular trip.

WHAT THIS BOOK IS ABOUT

This is not a book about executing a business strategy flawlessly. This book is about creating authentic total experiences that express an organization's core vision and values so integrally and seamlessly governed by an authentic, core vision that you truly set yourself apart from everyone else in your space. Customers want to do business with you, regardless of the price. Employees want to work for you because of your high performance standards and your vision of what your company offers to the world. All your stakeholders want to work with you because of what you stand for, and because you consistently and dependably deliver on your value proposition.

You will own your place in the market not by how well you execute your strategy but by how well you live out your authenticity in the expression of total experiences that touch your customers, your employees, your community, your vendors—any and all who come into contact with your organization. Those customers who demand a do-over will be coming back to you because they want more of what you have to offer. You'll have no problem delivering it —and this book will show you exactly how to make that happen.

In this book I will introduce you to a tried and true process for creating (or reimagining) an enterprise that delivers precisely the authentic set of experiences that set you apart from everyone else. Here's a rundown:

Chapter 1: Authenticity. This chapter explores the competitive and operational advantages associated with establishing your own authentic enterprise, specifically in keeping with the unique vision you share with all your stakeholders.

Chapter 2: Experience Matters. No matter what the nature of your organization might be, your authenticity is expressed through the experiences of all the people who come into contact with it. This chapter outlines the nine rules of great experiences and how they show up to your stakeholders.

Chapter 3: What Is Total Experience Design™? When you look at your organization's offerings in terms of a total framework of experiences in the realm of the 4P Model™ (Perception, People, Products and Services, Place), you are able to see how they interlock with each other to create what is known as *total experience design.*

Chapter 4: Go Big or Don't Bother. The pursuit of authenticity and total experience design demands a full-out commitment from the leadership so that all the stakeholders feel supported as they embark on this adventure. This chapter challenges you to double-check your true readiness in this endeavor.

Chapter 5: Discover. This chapter launches the 5D Process™ (Discover, Dream, Define, Design, Deliver) that is designed to help you and your team visualize the same ideal and authentic organization and take action to get there. The first D, Discover, shows you how to assess your current situation before you start taking action toward your ideal future.

Chapter 6: Dream. This is the chance to fully explore your organizational creativity and innovation. By following the exercises outlined in this chapter, you and your stakeholders build a shared, vivid, multisensory idea of what your enterprise will be, what it will stand for, and who it will serve. This shared vision will powerfully carry your team forward during the energetic, even uncertain times ahead.

Chapter 7: Define. Now that you know where you are, what your current conditions are, and where you want to go, it is time to identify all the gaps and conditions that keep you from realizing your dream right this very minute. Don't be dismayed by the number of gaps you and your team might identify. It means that you have set the bar high, so your ultimately transformed organization will be an inspiring example of what you are capable of when you establish your authentic dream and achieve it.

Chapter 8: Design. Every enterprise and organization undergoing its authentic transformation will have its own design process to initiate. Still, there are common leadership considerations around supporting your people as they begin designing all the ways to close those gaps that they discovered in the Define phase.

Chapter 9: Deliver. At last! Completion is in sight. Still, you need to track your progress, measure your results, and understand how to continue to lead your people as they are finding their footing in this new environment. And, by the way: completion may be in sight, but don't think you are finished yet. Your journey to authenticity never really ends.

PROLOGUE:
A TALE OF TWO DOCTORS

THE OFFICE OF DR. GREGORY LARSON

"As I said, ma'am, Dr. Larson is a busy man," said the harried nurse on the other end of the line. "I understand that this is your first time, but he can't see you until three weeks from Tuesday, and that's only if I juggle a few things on his calendar. . . ." The ad that led Barbara Evans to make this call had described Dr. Gregory Larson and his staff as the top OB/GYN practice in the area, with the newest and best-equipped women's clinic in the city. It also proclaimed in large, bold type that Dr. Larson was "welcoming new patients."

Three weeks later, Barbara sets out for her first prenatal appointment with Dr. Larson. The receptionist has provided sketchy directions to the center, and after two wrong turns, Barbara finally spots the large, modern medical office building with a huge parking garage. After crawling through the full lower levels, looking for a parking spot, Barbara finally finds a space on the sixth level on the side of the garage farthest away from the medical building's entrance. Glancing at her watch, Barbara realizes that she's seconds away from being late. She sprints toward the building entry.

Inside the clinic's brightly lit lobby, Barbara's eyes adjust to the glare of light bouncing off of the highly polished marble, which seems to cover every surface. Between the harried office workers scurrying to and fro, Barbara spies a sour-faced woman sitting behind an imposing reception desk in the center of the grand space. As Barbara approaches the desk, but before she can open her mouth, the woman jabs a finger in the air, brusquely pointing Barbara to a bank of elevators. The elevator that Barbara boards is playing the same piped-in, canned music that she heard in the lobby, only this time too loudly.

Entering Dr. Larson's fifth-floor waiting room, Barbara sees rows of uncomfortable, straight-back chairs lining the walls and arranged back-to-back in the center of the room. After signing in and reassuring the clinic receptionist that, yes, she has insurance, she joins the 15 other patients, resigning herself to the fact that she's in for a wait—and wondering how comfortable these chairs will be in six months or so.

Forty-five minutes later, Barbara hears her name called, and she follows a nurse to a small, sterile exam room that smells of antiseptic. The nurse thrusts a folded, pink paper square into Barbara's hands and says, "Everything off. It ties in the back. Doctor will be in to see you shortly." As the door shuts behind the nurse, Barbara stares down at the paper gown in her hands and sighs to herself, "So, this is what it's like. . . ."

THE OFFICE OF DR. EMILY MALLOY AND ASSOCIATES

Across town that same morning, Lisa Cambridge, one month pregnant with her first child, checks in with the receptionist at Dr. Emily Malloy's office. Lisa had heard a radio commercial describing Dr. Malloy's patient-centered approach to caregiving, so she called for an appointment. The nurse who took Lisa's initial call patiently answered all her questions, gave clear directions to the office, and told her what to expect during her first visit. Dr. Malloy's office manager followed up a few days later by sending Lisa a welcome packet with a personal letter of introduction from Dr. Malloy, including instructions repeating the details of what Lisa could expect. The packet also provided clear directions, information on where to park, and a friendly, open invitation to call with any other questions.

It turns out that Lisa doesn't need the parking information, because upon reaching her destination, Lisa decides to let a valet park her car at no charge. The building's lobby features a small, glass-tiled fountain at its center, and the bubbling water offers a pleasant and soothing sound. Any nervousness Lisa feels begins to dissipate as she walks deeper into the lobby, in part due to the soft strains of violin music filling the air, along with the smell of freshly ground and brewed coffee. Lisa realizes the source of both is a café next to a bank of elevators. The café opens out onto a lovely garden, where office workers seem to be enjoying a morning cup before heading to work.

As Lisa moves on, a smiling woman in front of a small desk adjacent to the elevators says, "Good morning. How may I help you?" With the gracious demeanor of a concierge at a fine hotel, the receptionist welcomes Lisa, confirms that she is headed in the right direction, and invites her to visit the well-stocked resource center just off the lobby after her visit.

A receiving nurse greets Lisa warmly upon her arrival to Dr. Malloy's office, and immediately leads her to a pleasant, warm exam room filled with diffused, natural light. There is an overstuffed chair nestled in a corner of the room, with a small table bearing a vase of tulips and the latest issue of a parenting magazine. After changing into a soft cotton robe the nurse had given her, Lisa settles into the comfortable chair and smiles to herself as she thinks, "So, this is what it's like!"

Chapter 1

AUTHENTICITY

Today you are you! That is truer than true. There is no one alive who is you-er than you.

Dr. Seuss

On March 28, 2008, *Time* magazine published a cover article package entitled "10 Ideas That Are Changing the World." Coming in at #7 was "Synthetic Authenticity." At first glance, this word combination might appear to be an oxymoron in that *synthetic* is often confused with fake—which, with very few exceptions, is typically presumed to be inauthentic. However, *synthetic* can also be used to describe the "combination of parts or elements so as to create a whole," which is, actually, a core responsibility of every CEO and leader of organizations, communities, and even families. Under the guidance of visionary leaders, any organization stands to blossom and achieve its potential through true authenticity—being true to itself. And the experiences that manifest this authenticity to everyone who comes into contact with the organization can and indeed should be intentionally created.

Leaders who take on the challenge of intentionally determining what is true to their organizations are joining a growing movement of product and service providers who want to stand above the crowd and achieve market differentiation based on the unique characteristics of their values, people, products, services, and even their place.

Although the pursuit of authenticity may help leaders come to an understanding as to what makes their enterprises truly unique, real differentiation happens only after all the elements of a *total experience,* or those interactions all of your stakeholders have with your organization, are identified and put into action. It's only when you achieve this level of differentiation through an integrated, intentional design of all those *total experience* ingredients that the playing field truly belongs to you. Then you won't compete based on price—*you will compete based on a shared ideal of what can be real and wonderful.*

In this context, authenticity emerges after all the key stakeholders in the organization create and agree upon a shared vision and how that vision can be *authentically experienced* in the form of real-life interactions and behaviors by everyone associated with the organization:

- What are the organization's values and how are they expressed through the decisions, choices, and behaviors of all its people?
- What can the clients and customers reliably expect as a result of doing business with this organization?
- What emotional experience can the clients and customers count on while associating with this organization?
- Which clients and customers does the organization aspire to serve and what are these buyers' specific characteristics and needs?
- What is the nonnegotiable level of quality that the customers can depend on in the organization's products and services?

The answers to these and other questions drive authentic experience, which, in turn, elevates an enterprise above the competitive playing field.

Authentic experience in this context doesn't just happen. It takes vision, planning, and mindful synthesis to bring all the selected elements of an organization together to create that whole. And those who have attained this goal discover that their work is more rewarding, their clients more in alignment with their vision and values, and their business conversations more inspiring for everyone concerned.

WHY AUTHENTICITY, AND WHY NOW?

In recent years, after a long run of prosperity that encouraged exuberant and imaginative businesses, we've seen a rash of headlines detailing businesses breaking faith with their stakeholders. This is an era that is producing deep skepticism within the populace in terms of business and government.

When it comes right down to it, any business is based upon an exchange between buyer and seller, the success of which can be greatly ensured for both parties if the exchange is built on trust. And these days, it seems as if trust is in short supply, as companies and organizations that stakeholders thought were being well run or properly managed, were, in fact, not.

Whether it was unbridled corporate greed that caused things to go awry, forcing government to step in to try and save the day, or sheer incompetence, we may never know for sure. But one thing is certain: our economy, our businesses, and in fact, our way of life as we know it is different now than it used to be. Things will continue to change and evolve. Things could always get worse—organizations, businesses, and even entire industries could fail to learn from this economic tsunami and continue their greedy, manipulative, and/or untrustworthy ways, or this economic evolution could set us on a path that leads toward organizations striving to offer their best and most authentic selves to a public hungry for it. It seems as if we may have hit a universal reset button, where many of us are asking, "What's important to me now?" Consumers are wondering how they want to use those last few dollars in their wallets. Entrepreneurs may be questioning exactly how they want to bring their new ideas to market in a way that is lasting and sustainable. Business leaders are saying, "Well, it's up from the ashes—where do we begin?" Because the world is now connected in ways we never dreamed possible, we have seen how our actions, whether they're based on avarice or altruism, can impact companies, economies, and communities far beyond our own. Don't we owe it to those connections, as well as to our own organizations, to jump on the chance to do it differently, and better, this time around?

The organizations and the brands that have and will stand the test of time are the ones that truly understand and celebrate who they are, and don't try to be or offer what they're not, who connect with all of their stakeholders on this basis, and thus become organizations their stakeholders can trust. And when their authentic offerings to those stakeholders are made on an emotional, multisensory, even aspirational level, then these experiences will be embraced as an invitation to belong, rather than simply as an opportunity to make a sale. This is when the customers become loyal beyond reason—when they connect with an organization on an emotional and even spiritual level.

This is what marketing expert Seth Godin calls belonging to a tribe— individuals who have voluntarily subscribed to your special world either for the time it takes to make a quick transaction, or to experience, for months, if not years, a rewarding relationship in your community. Customers and stakeholders identify with some aspect of who you are, what your organization stands for, and what it has to offer. Or they identify with each other. Whatever that connecting essence is, a world is created, relationships are established, loyalty flourishes, and your enterprise thrives. That's real.

In an era of dissembling and marginalizing the truth, it's quite possible that a simple, straight-forward business plan based on the single premise of determining what is authentic about your organization, and then making your authenticity manifest in everything you do, is what will help elevate you above the crowd, and keep you there far into the future. In some industries, just having the reputation of living your authenticity by keeping your promises puts you miles ahead of your competitors.

These rapid-fire, hair-trigger times demand that CEOs and other organizational leaders become change masters. Some companies change their strategies with the turnover (or overturn) of their top-tier executives. Some companies change their strategies as frequently as every quarter or even a couple of times a fiscal period. The smart leaders use this mandate to change as an opportunity to build their companies' core essence into that which is authentic, durable, and sustainable. It's not a question of tweaking a brand identity here, repainting the lobby there, or adding a new training program for the staff. It's about intentionally and deeply integrating all the essential, nonnegotiable elements of what defines a company in the eyes of its stakeholders—what we at Kahler Slater call *total experience design*.

As a nation, we have witnessed tragic, knuckle-headed business transformations that ended up being one last gasp before the doors were chained. But the transformations that become truly legendary are the ones that start out by reaching deep into the DNA of a company's very being (its culture, its values, its people, its very processes) to make every single decision purposeful and answerable to the larger question of "Who do we want to be now, tomorrow, ever after?" "Who do we want to be to our customers, even when we're operating on only one engine?" "What kinds of customers do we want to retain as we're moving full steam ahead?" And, "Exactly how do we want these values to show up as our customers' experience of us?"

An organization's authentic essence, for good or for bad, is real, and comes across in ways large and small, planned and spontaneous. Authenticity, or the lack thereof, is manifest in everything the organization says and does and is:

- Its perception and image in the marketplace
- The products it makes and/or the services it offers
- The people who make the products and/or deliver the services
- Its place—that physical presence, which should clearly represent the organization's personality and values in all details—the location, the interior design, workflows, etc.

The organizational leaders with whom we work recognize the essential value in manifesting their Organizational Vision in everything they do, and on a consistent basis, day in and day out. They're looking for a way to turn a vision into experiences that can be operationalized, executed, felt, owned, and, ultimately, valued by their clients, employees, and communities—all of their stakeholders. And when that experience is authentic to the DNA that makes up each unique business and organization, *marketplace differentiation* is created and sustained for the long haul. In this way, the enterprise rises above the clutter and noise of price competition, the time- and resource-wasting distraction of chasing the wrong customers, and losing focus on what is really important to the business.

With that authentic core in place, *you* are your own category, so *you* can name your terms. And so the next step is discovering exactly how that authenticity shows up in the experiences of all your stakeholders. That is where a good idea is transformed into something real that everyone who comes into contact with your business can consistently count on.

Big ideas and exceptional experiences—and the transformations they drive—change the world and set new standards that inspire passion and genius in others and lead to further transformations.

So, What Is Authenticity, Anyway?

The subject of authenticity has befuddled philosophers, writers, and artists for years. Even Plato with his cave kept himself awake wondering if what we perceive is really real or just an illusion as filtered through our own personal layers of perception. The Belgian artist, René Magritte, with his famous painting, *Ceci n'est pas une pipe,* felt compelled to remind us that the oil on his canvas only *represented* a pipe. It wasn't a real pipe. ("If I had written on my picture 'this is a pipe,'" said Magritte, "I would have been lying."[1]) So you had better not try to light it. The museum alarms, not to mention the sprinkler system, would go off. And that would be just really embarrassing.

If we wanted to get down to the purest, most basic essence of authenticity, we'd enter the realm of quantum physics. This desk that's holding up my computer right now is nothing but a swarming mass of pulsing atoms, as firm and as stable as gelatin (probably even less so, seeing as how gelatin is also a swarming mass of pulsing atoms). The book you're holding right now is also a swarming mass of atoms. What's holding everything up and helping to keep its shape? That's also a question for the philosophers and physicists. Is my desk authentically solid? I sure hope so, because I'm counting on it to see me through in completing this book.

Perhaps authenticity changes its meaning depending on its context. For instance, art appraisers, archaeologists, museum curators, even antiquities smugglers (and forgers) have an intense interest in what is fake and what is true to its purported provenance. A forgery is a forgery—even if the fraudulent piece itself dates back several centuries before Christ.

"Is she for real?" Chances are whoever asked this question wasn't referring to the metaphysical state of this person. Rather, the question, which we've probably all asked, or which has been asked about us, refers to the person's authenticity—is she genuine? Just as this question is asked about people, so too, can it be asked about organizations. And the answer is perhaps made most evident by observing behavior. Is this person or organization behaving in a way that matches the messages they send? Does she walk her talk? Is the way in which I interact or experience this organization consistent with who they say they are, what they say they offer to me, and the promises that they make? If the answer is yes, then our belief in the authenticity of that individual or organization is more likely to be confirmed than if our observations or experiences are otherwise.

For purposes of this book, we'll leave behind the philosophical and metaphysical discussions about what authenticity is or isn't and instead focus on *organizational authenticity*—the values, purpose, and passions that are at the heart of why any business, institution, or organization exists in the first place, and which drive what the organization is trying to achieve, as well as how it goes about doing it. It might be easy to see how this definition applies to a nonprofit organization that is, for instance, all about trying to make the world a greener place. And you can see how, if it is to make manifest this organizational authenticity, everything it does should be done with the sustainability of the environment in mind—can you imagine, for instance, getting a fundraising letter from such an organization that wasn't printed on recycled paper? Wouldn't that make you question its authenticity as a group committed to sustainability?

Although all businesses exist, arguably, to make a profit, a business like Google, at its core, exists not only to make a buck, but to create technological innovations. And everything it does, from the people it hires to the operational procedures it has in place, to the products it makes, all are created and executed around this critical tenet.

In his book, *Whoosh: Business in the Fast Lane,* consultant Tom McGehee talks about Walmart as an example of organizational authenticity when he writes,

> Think of Walmart's "every day low prices." Ever been to their corporate headquarters? Their plastic chairs and linoleum-floored offices may not be comfortable, but they sure are consistent with their message to customers. When their corporate teams travel, they fly cheap, stay at standard hotels, and often sleep two to a room. . . . Their purpose is consistent with the way they work, how they act, what they value.[2]

Walmart is about frugality. It shows in everything they do. If you work at Walmart, you know what to focus on. And if you shop at Walmart, you know what to expect.

So, although this book won't be looking too closely at the essential *nature* of authenticity, we will be focusing on the *synthesis* of authenticity, especially as it relates to the decisions you make about how your stakeholders experience your enterprise—be it a business or a community service or a hospital.

In this book, we'll talk about *authenticity* from the perspective of it being an agreement between an enterprise and its stakeholders about what experiences will be expected and delivered. Authenticity doesn't mean much if it can't be manifest in the everyday experiences of your organization. If what you say you are doesn't hold up to how you behave, you're a fake. You're not walking your talk. And your stakeholders, who want and need more than ever these days to trust that you are who you say you are, will seek out some other organization or institution that is authentic, who they'll want to buy from, work for, and associate with.

How this authenticity is made manifest should not be left to chance, but rather can and should be intentionally designed down to the last detail. When you're manifesting your organizational authenticity, you need to commit yourself wholeheartedly to it. And then you will find stakeholders who are eager to be your partners in the experience delivery of what you have to offer.

The Advantages of Real

We've seen how much trouble businesses and organizations can get into when they slide off the rails of their own purported purpose. They're exposed for the frauds that they've always been or the fools that they have become. And as economic hardships continue to strip away the layers of insulation between them and the hard light of public scrutiny, their options for finessing disappear. Blogs, Twitter, YouTube, and 24-hour news only increase their liabilities for exposure.

According to a June 2009 McKinsey Quarterly report, a survey of global senior executives the previous March found that the majority surveyed agreed "that public trust in business and commitment to free markets had deteriorated." The report showed that the 2009 Edelman Trust Barometer survey indicated that "62 percent of respondents, across 20 countries, say that they 'trust corporations less now than they did a year ago.'" The article goes on to note,

> The breadth and depth of today's reputational challenge is a consequence not just of the speed, severity, and unexpectedness of recent economic events but also of underlying shifts in the reputation environment that have been under way for some time. Those changes

include the growing importance of Web-based participatory media, the increasing significance of nongovernmental organizations (NGOs) and other third parties, and declining trust in advertising. Together, these forces are promoting wider, faster scrutiny of companies and rendering traditional public-relations tools less effective in addressing reputational challenges.[3]

Henceforth, it will be action and not spin that builds and sustains a good reputation.

Authenticity, or being genuine and real, is a worthy goal. And it's not foreign territory. You may already be more authentic in the delivery of your products and services than you might think. And if that's the case, then your next challenge is to leverage your authenticity to its full advantage to your enterprise. But first, it will probably be helpful to have a full understanding of all the advantages of authenticity.

You have more control over your world. What you have to offer your stakeholders will be fabricated to some extent. So you might as well be the one who does the manufacturing. This isn't to say that you have to actually build your product yourself (which might not be so easy if you're selling imaging machines or cars), but you can build the *experience* of engaging with that product, starting from the moment your potential customers start considering it. When you choose to lead your enterprise with vision, you can create an authentic world that is real to everyone who participates in it—even if it's just for the time it takes to buy a pack of gum.

When you claim that power to design your authentic world, *you* can make the critical decisions that ultimately manifest that world for everyone associated with it. This is not to imply that the design of your enterprise should be a megalomaniacal exercise in dictatorship. But because you are the visionary leader, the dream starts with you. And the team that helps you manifest that dream will be the one that is picked because of a fit of values, authenticity, and a shared sense of what's right and what's possible.

Clarity around your particular idea of authenticity will make difficult decisions and choices easier to make. Your vision will have certain ground rules and expectations attached to it. When you're clear about what kind of world you want to create for your stakeholders, you will also know what won't work in that world. You will spot disconnects between your dream for the future manifestation of your authenticity and your current organizational experiences and reality, and you can start closing those gaps immediately. Because you're now clear on what *authentic* means to you, you will experience a sense of urgency to remove those disconnects promptly, which will ultimately be of service to your stakeholders. Your clients will know they can count on you to deliver your promise. And your employees will know that they can count on you to give them what they need to succeed in their jobs.

This may mean that you must reluctantly release a cherished, long-term employee. Or perhaps hold a critical position open until you find the perfect candidate. Or perhaps you'll be forced to recall a product that no longer represents your new standards for quality. Or you may have to terminate a relationship with long-standing clients because your values no longer match. The decisions may be painful, but their necessity will be absolutely clear. The clarity of authenticity will govern your decisions in those difficult moments, and you will have the confidence that your stakeholders will support you in the service of your shared vision made manifest.

Your competition will be immaterial. When you design your enterprise based on your unique and authentic vision and in collaboration with all your stakeholders—including your potential customers—you are developing a one-of-a-kind offering to your community. This is called *differentiation,* and it quite literally sets you apart from your more ho-hum, so-called competitors who only think that they're playing the same game you are.

When you are a one-of-a-kind enterprise, your more run-of-the-mill competitors drop away very quickly because they are competing with each other based on price and playing a loser's game, because the only direction they can move is down. You're left with truly worthy opponents who compete with you based on ideas and quality and customer service levels. And when you compete with them, the only direction you can move successfully is up—improving on all those touchpoints that make your enterprise the one your stakeholders choose, because they can. If they go with your competition, it might be disappointing but in the long run it will be okay. These potential customers and even employees are attracted to aspects of your competitors' world that you have no interest in. You may even discover, as you'll see later when you read about benchmarking, that you might work in collaboration with your competitors now and then, each of you bringing your unique strengths to expand upon your mutual understanding of the shared market space.

Don't think that whatever business or endeavor you're in is too ordinary to be differentiated. According to Jack Trout in his book *Differentiate or Die,* "the diaper biz is one of the most heavily patented in the annals of the Patent and Trademark Office," with 1,000 different patents to "guard everything from the Velcro fastener tabs to the amount of elastic around the legs." If diapers can find their extraordinary niche 1,000 different ways, surely there's a way to make your enterprise stand out.[4]

Trout goes on to quote Ted Levitt's 1991 book, *Thinking About Management:*

> Differentiation is one of the most important strategic and tactical activities in which companies must constantly engage. It is not discretionary. And everything can be differentiated, even so-called "commodities" such as cement, copper, wheat, money, air cargo, marine insurance. There is no such thing as a commodity, only people who act and think like commodities.[5]

You won't have to be perfect. Some will tell you that once you're identified as offering an authentic experience to your customers, there will be a bull's-eye on your back. You're tempting fate. You're going to fall off the pedestal you've so cleverly built for yourself, and you will be shamed in front of the entire world. Actually, just the opposite is true. True authenticity breeds enduring loyalty from all the stakeholders in your community. They will stand by you, even in those moments where you slip up (witness the engine fire on the *SeaDream*—see the Introduction for the full story). Your commitment to delivering authentic experiences is a commitment to an organizing principle or value that will drive all your business decisions and choices. It's not a public declaration that you're perfect. People get that.

It is also not a public declaration that you have set your business in amber, never to change or evolve. Although the authentic nature of your business may never change (your values and your purpose, for instance), the authentic *experience* of that nature is completely updatable and transformable through the years. The experiences that your business offers your customers and stakeholders are most certainly subject to modification as time and circumstances change. And if you engineer those experiences now, according to your defined sense of who you want to be and what values you want to represent, any future transformations of those experiences will be absolutely consistent with who you are and have been all along.

You will enjoy being held to your promise. In his book, *Emotional Branding: The New Paradigm for Connecting Brands to People,* Marc Gobe writes:

> One single idea—especially if it involves a great brand concept—can change a company's entire future. . . . It is the emotional aspect of products and their distribution systems that will be the key difference. . . . Corporations must take definite steps toward building stronger connections and relationships which recognize their customers as partners.[6]

When your enterprise aligns all its decisionmaking and choices with that one great idea or vision, your tribe will find you. They will be able to quickly spot what you stand for and what your commitment is to everyone associated with your organization. And then they will invite others into the group. And, as long as you are sincere in keeping your vision alive and viable, your tribe will hold you up and support you. They will hold you to your promise. This will actually be an imposition you welcome because you know these are "your" people and that they see the vision you're seeing. They are your co-collaborators.

No matter what your enterprise does or offers, unless you're dealing in those random atoms, you are making something new to offer the world. You have the choice to make it fraudulent, in which case you are limiting the prospects, potential, and even longevity of your dream. Or you can make it real, in which case you are defined only by your values and the details of your dream.

How does real actually manifest itself? Through experiences, of course. Living out your authenticity isn't easy, but if your stakeholders can't experience it, then just how real is it?

Once you identify how your organizational authenticity will be expressed through experiences, that's when you are truly in business. All the following advantages are in your favor.

Alignment

When you have identified all the ways experience authentically represents your business, you can intentionally engineer all those essential business elements to best work together in support of your core authenticity. Nothing should be out of tune, out of step, or out of place with the core promise of your enterprise. You will attract the kinds of customers and employees who share your values. And they will be intrinsically motivated to behave accordingly.

When you are working with the clients who are a perfect fit with your business—the people who want what it is that you offer and how you offer it—everyone wins. You are able to do your best work, which is satisfying for you, your employees, and for your customers. This is where you find you are also doing your most profitable work, having the most fun, and where you are the most innovative, because you, your employees, and your customers trust and understand each other enough to allow each other to try new things.

Depending on the business that you're in, you could also be in a better position to help your clients do a better job serving *their* clients. You're doing well by helping your customers do well.

By identifying the many ways your authenticity is expressed through the experiences of everyone who comes into contact with your organization, you are creating a business ecosystem of interdependent relationships and expectations that have far-reaching effects, beyond just the immediate transaction.

Performance

Most everyone has probably had the unfortunate experience of expecting one level of performance based on a company's marketing message but actually receiving a much lower level of service. It's disappointing, disheartening, and disillusioning. It's unmistakable to customers, and generally businesses have only one chance to fulfill their marketing promise before the customer takes the business elsewhere. But employees—especially the high-value, high-performing people—are also discouraged by the promise gap. And when these people are repeatedly assaulted by the negative effects of the authenticity disconnect, businesses lose the value of their performance as well. They either suffer high turnover rates or otherwise great employees "quitting in place."

Only a deeply rooted commitment to the many details that go into authentic experience will result in a performance that offers that experience in fact. That's when you get high performance. When you and your employees work together to design the many aspects of your business specifically according to the experiences that best express your authenticity, your entire organization is going to be high-performing in a truly integrated way.

With everyone collaborating to identify and articulate the specifics of how to carry out your authentic vision (which is the *total experience design* process we will discuss in this book), you have communal buy-in as to the performance standards you expect. With the consensus-building power of the total experience design process, your staff will create the authentic experiences that manifest your organizational authenticity, and they will own the responsibility for manifesting those experiences through all their behaviors and self-imposed quality standards. Execution of the Organizational Vision made manifest through these experiences will become second nature to them; and they won't need any laminated cards to remind them of what your specific and authentic quality performance looks like in their interactions with your customers and each other. The entire group will become self-policing as they excitedly work together (and support one another) to create the business of everyone's dreams.

As the leader, you may have been the one to originate the core authentic idea around which your enterprise will be built. But it will be your people who will operationalize that idea and turn your organization into one that will consistently deliver the performance quality that you promise.

The Competitive Advantage of Differentiation

There are few enterprises that are so unique that they can't be duplicated by competitors who are willing to deliver the same service or product at cheaper prices. Therefore, as a business leader, you have a choice: You can compete by lowering your prices and suffering the pinching effects of ever-shrinking profit margins. Or you can compete on the basis of delivering products and services in a way that is authentic to your unique organization. You will do so with the help of impassioned employees serving enthusiastic customers who appreciate the intrinsic value of personally belonging to your unique community. Both choices are perfectly acceptable, but which sounds more profitable, satisfying, and fun to you?

If you base your enterprise on authenticity—and all the experiences that bring that authenticity to life—you own your own playing field. There is no one who can successfully compete head-to-head with you based on all your essential differentiating factors: price, quality, performance, and the unique experience of doing business with you and your company.

When you design your enterprise based on the elements that go into authentic experience, you have the corner on your own market. No one can fake or copy your unique, distinctive essence. Your business is as unique as a fingerprint. Customers who try one of your direct competitors (or copiers) in search of the exact experience they have had with you will walk away disappointed. And they will walk right back to you, wiser for having experienced the difference first hand.

Chapter 2

EXPERIENCE MATTERS

In wisdom gathered over time I have found that every experience is a form of exploration.

Ansel Adams

The authenticity of an enterprise begins as the brainchild of the entrepreneur or its leaders. It often starts as an undefined, generalized sense of what the ideal world might be that the enterprise creates (even if that *world* is as small as, say, a candy store or restaurant). And then, iteration after iteration, the details are layered on to bring the original concept to life. Still, no matter how detailed that concept might become, it's just a vague notion until it's rolled out to the world and all stakeholders are invited to test its promises. At this point, the internalized ideal of what the originators might have labeled as *authentic* becomes externalized and proven through how the customers, employees, neighbors, vendors, and even competitors actually *experience* their interaction with the organization.

It's through actual experiences when the originators' vision and dreams are made manifest—or they fall apart altogether. And, unless the entire tapestry of the enterprise is woven against the same tight, unified backing of authenticity, that tapestry can unravel devastatingly quickly with the pull of one unfortunate, bad experience thread. You can proclaim your sincerity and your commitment to authenticity all you want. But if your stakeholders' experiences of your enterprise don't match your story, you've got nothing but a hollow promise.

For instance, my colleague Martha tells the story of the day she took her car into the dealer in Santa Fe for service under some very tight time constraints. She drives a car that belongs to a brand that promotes truly high-end customer service. And in the four years Martha has owned the car—a top-of-the-line model of an already expensive brand—her experience of her local dealership has been flawless. Even though she only visits the dealership a few times a year, the staff know her by name. She always feels as if she's returning to a club, with a waiting room that is designed for comfort and the opportunity to meet other congenial owners of the same brand of automobile.

On this particular occasion, Martha needed to squeeze her regular service inside an extremely busy day. And, when scheduling her appointment, she made extra certain that she would be back in her office in time for a 12:30 conference call. True to the nature of this dealership and its service-oriented staff, everyone was put on alert, and they put her car at the head of the line. "It was like watching an organ transplant team in action," Martha recalls. "Not a motion was wasted, everyone was pulling together to get that car in and out in record time. It was a wonder to behold. And, based on my previous experiences there, it was what I expected."

When her car was finished, she picked up her keys and flew out of the service center with an hour to spare, gushing the entire time, "I just love you guys!" "We love you back!" she heard as she headed for her car in the parking lot. And that's where the trouble began.

While her car was parked, another car had stopped directly behind it, blocking Martha's ability to back out. A salesperson was leaning into the window of the other car, trying to convince an elderly couple to buy a new car rather than simply have their current one serviced. (The salesperson, who worked in the sales department and not in the service department, wasn't privy to the fact that Martha was on a tight schedule. And he didn't seem to care that he was inconveniencing an established customer while trying to recruit two new ones.) This is how the conversation went:

Martha: Excuse me! Could you move your car? I'm in a hurry and need to be on my way.

Salesperson: Yeah. Yeah. In a minute. (And then he returned to chatting up the shanghaied couple.)

A couple of minutes later, Martha: No, really, I have got to go.

Salesperson (straightening up to full height): Hey! Have some manners, why don't you!

After a few more minutes, the other car finally moved, and Martha was able to pull out. But the story isn't over yet. As she inched her way out of the parking lot, the salesperson crossed in front of her car. She rolled down the window and said in a friendly voice, "What's your name?"

Salesperson: What's it to you? You writing a book?

Martha, truthfully: As a matter of fact, yes.

Salesperson: Good. Make it a mystery.

The salesperson had the misfortune of underestimating Martha's passion for and expectation of high-quality customer experience, not to mention overlooking the fact that she was now paused directly in front of the service door. This was the very same door she had just flown out of, happily energized by her appreciation of the dealership's commitment to superior customer care. She calmly turned off the ignition, got out of the car, and walked back through that door, only this time with an entirely different message for the service desk. She explained what had just happened. And then went on her way to make it to her appointment on time.

It would be another month or so before she would learn that that salesperson was fired that very afternoon.

It was actually that dealership's track record in providing top-notch customer *experiences* that saved their relationship with this loyal customer. To Martha, her perception of the authenticity of the brand would have been stopped cold by the rudeness and selfishness of the salesperson—had it not been for a history of consistently excellent experiences with the same dealership's service staff. Those accumulated experiences had combined to make a *relationship* with these individuals—a relationship that Martha remains willing to pay a premium for, even though she could probably get the same tasks accomplished at a local franchise down the street at a fraction of the expense. And this history of authentic experiences transformed her into a partner, with a shared stake in the enterprise's success.

Had the experience of the dealership been spotty, indifferent, or consistently at odds with its paid advertising and marketing slogans, she could have quickly forgotten the extreme, high level of customized attention she had just received. But she would have remembered that one negative experience with the rude salesperson that had the potential to ruin the entire morning for her. She probably would not have told the service staff what had happened with the salesperson. But she would have told all her friends.

As for the rest of the dealership, how motivated would they continue to be to provide differentiated, personalized service if they were habitually undermined by a management approach that placed more value on making a new sale than on retaining current customers? They can go out of their way to provide excellent service, knowing that their commitment to this level of excellence will be supported all the way up the management chain.

For this particular car maker and its affiliated dealerships, the way the customers experience their service is as essential as the car's reputation for safety and style. These owners willingly pay a premium for the experience of being treated in a way that is in concert with that car maker's brand. Martha says that though it was too bad that someone should get fired as a result of an egregious breach of the brand promise, she recognizes the fact that the dealership's treatment of her in the past (her *experience*) made her one of its brand champions. She is happy to be a citizen of this brand's tribe. So a glitch in the experience every now and then is forgiven when the overall expectation of experience remains consistent with the stated brand of quality service, product, and people.

Brand is much more than a name or a logo, slogan, or even reputation. Rather, it's what the business owner wants the end user to *experience consistently and over time.* Whether you are running a hospital, hotel, restaurant, coffee shop, or nonprofit organization, to set yourself apart in an increasingly crowded marketplace, everything about the way you do business should be a unified statement of who you are at the most authentic core of your organization and manifest what you care about the most. If something is out of place in this regard, you may not necessarily know it—at least not right away—but your customers sure will. And, unless your relationship is firmly established with your customers, they might not tell you. But they may take their business elsewhere, especially if your competitors promise a more consistently dependable and authentic experience. By paying attention to all the many ways your business or organization connects with your key stakeholders—the *touchpoints,* which we'll explore in Chapter 3—you will attract and keep employees who want to work with you and clients who intentionally want to do business with you. Why? Because you will be unlike anyone or anything else.

Your track record of delivering successful and quality experiences is what will differentiate you from any other enterprise that might aspire to be a competitor. You will develop a loyal following not because you are the least expensive option, but because the experience of engaging with you is predictable and consistent. Your bond with your stakeholders will be an emotional one more than one based on the bottom line. They choose to engage with you because of the experience you promise to them—not necessarily because of a savings you might represent (unless, that is, savings are a part of your experience offering).

The experiences you're offering should not be cookie–cutter. They should be unique to both you and the stakeholders you're serving. Still, there are some universal truths around the principle of experience as a differentiating factor:

RULE #1: EVERY ORGANIZATION CAN BE EXPERIENTIAL

Experience isn't merely some high-concept approach to designing cutting-edge boutique companies. Go into the most ordinary place of business and you're entering its world of experiences. A convenience store, for example, has a set of experiences attached to it: the search for the sign marked

Restrooms and the fervent hope that it will lead you to a clean facility. A trip to the florist where the fragrance from the blossoms seems to ride lightly on the refrigerated air. Your biannual visit to the dentist where (in contrast) just the anticipation of novocaine starts your adrenaline pumping.

Every encounter—intentionally designed, or left to chance—is layer upon layer of sensory and behavioral cues that tell stakeholders whether they are going to receive what you offered and whether they will be treated the way they want to be while they're engaging in precisely the kind of transaction for which they came to you.

RULE #2: AN INTENTIONALLY DESIGNED EXPERIENCE CAN BE AUTHENTIC, TOO

It's tempting to assume that truly authentic experiences just happen; they sprout organically from the heart, mind, and good intentions of their artisan founders (with 15 percent of all proceeds donated to charity, and you save money if you bring your own shopping bags).

But intentionally designed experiences, those that come from conference rooms, sprung from the brainstorming minds of well-paid executives, can be just as authentic and emotionally powerful as any passion-driven idea humbly hatched at a kitchen table. You can even send the designed set of experiences through your big company marketing machine tests and measures (surveys, focus groups, etc.) and still be authentic in your commitment to create and deliver your service or product to your customers.

The main question is whether you and your team (including your customers and stakeholders) can sustain your passion for your vision to such a detailed extent that you can reasonably commit to delivering that set of experiences on a consistent and regular basis. That commitment is where the power of your authenticity lies.

Authenticity is how you decide what you want to be to your marketplace. Experience is when your customers decide whether they want what you have to offer them in that marketplace. If you have to design that deliverable down to the smallest detail, so much the better. With each layer of detail you put down, your offering will be that much clearer. And you will be able to attract the customers who have been looking for you all this time.

RULE #3: EVERYONE HAS A ROLE IN EXPERIENCE DELIVERY

It can be very easy to get so overwhelmed with the entire scope of creating an enterprise founded on authenticity that you decide to simply toss this *authenticity thing* over to marketing, PR, or corporate communications. Your marketing and communications people are essential to the process, absolutely. But they can't carry the torch alone. If you are planning a complete transformation of your enterprise, or starting from scratch, you are building a new relationship with your stakeholders. And as such, everyone inside your organization must be a key player in this initiative. As we'll see in the next chapter, as you design your new endeavor, you'll be addressing the touchpoints between your enterprise and all its stakeholders that extend far beyond your brand messaging, the vocabulary you choose to use, the colors on your wall, and your press releases.

Those elements are important, to be sure, but they are just the *hello* in the process of building a fresh, sustainable, and authentic relationship with your stakeholders. The enduring relationship is built on consistently keeping that brand promise with everyone associated with your enterprise. And, to truly cover all those touchpoints, you must bring your entire team into the process. That way you're delivering the same authentic experience to everyone associated with your enterprise—from the first "hello" to "hello, how nice to see you again."

Even your stakeholders have a role in experience delivery. An organization truly and deeply committed to a well-articulated and authentic culture (with defined experiences to go along with it) becomes more like a club of like-minded members than a place of transaction. Your customers become members—citizens of a world you have created. And it's to their benefit to be *good* citizens of this world. They want your world to succeed because it's their world too, however briefly they might be in it with you.

Your world has norms, behaviors, and expectations of its citizens, just as any community does. And it's understood that everyone will behave themselves in order to continue to belong to that world. As citizens of your world, your stakeholders are partners with you in the mission of creating the experiences you have designed. They're active participants in these experiences, not just passive recipients of your service or user of your product.

If, like Martha, they find their actual experience to be out of whack with the promised experience, you're going to hear about it. And that's actually good news. They'll help you keep your vision on track, perhaps making your life a little difficult at times, but making your enterprise a success in the long run. Treat them as respected partners, and you'll get what you need to keep creating those experiences that make your enterprise ring true.

It's said that no one likes a critic. Unless, of course, that critic steers you away from making a bad commitment. Because of social media and easy access to review sites and blogs, word of mouth is king like never before. Instead of just being able to influence buying behaviors inside a relatively isolated neighborhood, which was the case only 15 years ago, one person can spread the word about your inauthenticity around the globe in less than the time it takes to power up your computer. Unhappy employees let it be known that their workplace isn't as great as you might think it is. Disgruntled customers have no trouble speaking their minds about what's wrong with the books, cameras, mixing bowls, or spray deodorant that they purchase.

Word of mouth keeps you authentic, whether you like it or not. So you can make your business life much easier by deciding what your authenticity is going to be and what behaviors will deliver the experiences that manifest that authenticity. You will be held to your promise—quite publicly. So what's your promise going to be?

RULE #4: EXPERIENCE IS NOT THEATER

In their book, *The Experience Economy: Work Is Theatre and Every Business a Stage,* authors Joseph Pine and James Gilmore assert that "business performances must rival those featured on Broadway and in ballparks."[1] For the average organization, that's a mighty high bar to reach for. And then, how much exertion is necessary to sustain that level of performance when all you want to do is provide your stakeholders with the best possible experiences that are authentic to you and everyone associated with your organization?

The very nature of theater is to deliver an illusion of reality in an unreal context. If that's the case, where is authenticity in the mix? If you think that you are able to project authentic caring and customer service through a deliberately crafted script that you require your staff to follow word for word, the only person you're kidding is yourself. Nothing highlights inauthenticity more than the tired, bored, or dispirited employee's hard haul toward acting pleasant, interested, or completely absorbed in the essential goal of making each and every customer insanely happy. Most people aren't stupid. Even as they're on the phone with a customer service rep, they can practically see the rep absorbed by a hangnail while robotically uttering, "How may I help you?"

Build your idea of delivering experiences based on your solidly authentic organizational foundation, and you can throw the scripts out the window. By understanding and making manifest your organizational authenticity, you will have a consistent, strong, integrated story of your organization and what it stands for to rely on to attract both high-performing employees, as well as customers who agree with your product/service offerings philosophy.

By being specific and real about who you are and what you offer to everyone associated with your enterprise, you're inviting all stakeholders to be your partners in a shared success story. The transaction will be successful because the customers who want what you have know they can reliably come to your place of business. You will be so certain about what kinds of experiences you want your stakeholders to have, that clarity will serve to attract the right kinds of potential employees and perhaps repel the ones who disagree with your vision (at least your clarity will make these people easier to spot in the recruitment process). People who *get* you will *find* you. And then no one needs a script to enforce the brand promise.

RULE #5: YOUR EMPLOYEES DESERVE THE SAME KINDS OF EXPERIENCES YOU OFFER YOUR STAKEHOLDERS

In the enterprise where there are authentic experiences being delivered, *offstage* isn't that different from *onstage*. It's just more private, away from the customers' world. As a visionary leader who cares about the experiences of everyone associated with your enterprise, you know it's important for your employees to be able to relax without worry of spoiling the experience for your customers and other outsiders (call them *guests* if you want, but it does- n't change the fact that they are paying customers who don't necessarily want to see behind the scenes).

The experience you want to keep intact is just that—an *experience,* not an illusion. As such, your employees deserve to have the same experiences and consideration that you're expecting them to give their customers. For instance, the break space you give them should be a natural transition from the *onstage* version of their working lives to the private *backstage* area. Clean. Well-lit. Organized, with a safe place to put their personal belongings. Com- fortable. Designed according to the same themes as the *onstage* version of the work environment. The finishes don't necessarily have to be as luxurious, but a drastic change can be destructive to your authentic culture. A transition from mahogany to plywood is a shock to any system and sends a message that as a leader you don't really mean what you say.

RULE #6: ATTENTION TO EXPERIENCE MAKES IT A LOT EASIER TO PLEASE YOUR STAKEHOLDERS

Clarity comes with your commitment to provide experiences based on your authenticity. When you know who you want to be in your market- place, your customers will know what to expect from you—right down to the last detail. As a result of your authentic specificity, you will attract the people who want what you have to offer (both employees and customers). And the others will pass you by. And that's okay. You can't please all the people, right?

Your customers are your partners in your success. They want you to do well, because it's important to them that they continue to have access to your service and product offerings. They become an extended board of directors, of sorts. They may not agree with every customer-service business decision you make. But assuming you're attracting the customers who agree with your fundamental premise and most of the details to manifest that premise, you can be confident that their opinions are worth listening to.

Your customers will want the kind of experiences you want to give them. So they will be more willing to give you the information, insight, and guidance you need to achieve your goals.

RULE #7: WHEN AUTHENTICITY IS TIGHTLY WOVEN, THE EXPERIENCE GAPS ARE GLARING

The marketing professionals call these *brand gaps*—those instances when the message and the reality of the experience just don't jive with each other. As a customer, you have surely experienced this yourself. A surly receptionist at a high-end spa who can barely unclench her jaw to say, "Can I help you?" Peeling paint on the walls of a hardware store. An upscale hotel that charges a hefty *resort fee,* but doesn't provide hot water in your room. How did that make you feel? Feeling ripped off is bad enough. But being played for a fool just adds to the injury, doesn't it?

Just because you say something is so, that doesn't make it so. In fact, the more you say something is so, and the disconnect in the experience points out otherwise, the more glaring those gaps will be, which will put you on the path to truly falling short of your ideal scenario. It's best to keep quiet until you are confident that all of your touchpoints have been assessed and designed to be what you want them to be—and say what you want them to say—about your organization.

RULE #8: THERE IS NO SUCH THING AS AN INDIFFERENT EXPERIENCE

The stakeholders who engage with your organization and never come back may seem indifferent to you, or at the very least invisible. But, unless they engaged with you for a once-in-a-lifetime transaction, such as buying their dream home or an engagement ring, or finally taking that around-the-world vacation, something went terribly wrong for those people who never return to you. And maybe that's okay because, as we just discussed, they may not be the right fit for your organization anyway.

But they were originally attracted to your place of business for a reason. They came with a specific set of expectations, even if those expectations were driven primarily by curiosity. So you're going to want to find out why they weren't attracted a second time. How were they disappointed? Did someone on your staff fail to fulfill the brand promise? Was the product disappointing? Is your place of business somehow off-putting?

If they're not already committed customers who consider themselves to be a member of your tribe, they may indeed be indifferent to your business and its prospects for success. But their indifference should not be immaterial to you. Not until you know exactly why they didn't subscribe to the tribe.

RULE #9: A BAD EXPERIENCE CAN BE FIXED

No organization is perfect, and no business can deliver successful total experiences to everyone all of the time. But that doesn't mean they shouldn't try, or that they shouldn't try to recover, and do so quickly, if things go south, even despite their best efforts.

It's Mother's Day, which means that you'll find my family in a restaurant having brunch. On one particular Mother's Day, we decide to try a new restaurant in town about which we've recently read a good review. The valet who parks our car upon arrival seems nice enough, as does the host who shows us to our table. The place is lovely, as expected—elegant, but comfortable, with warm, natural finishes and colors, and soft jazz playing in the background, adding to the relaxed mood. The smiling waitress answers our questions and pleasantly offers suggestions about what to order.

And when our drinks fail to arrive after 20 minutes, and our meal still hasn't arrived after another 30 minutes, the host arrives at our table bearing an embarrassed smile and what seems to be a sincere apology. The restaurant is new, and they're having some operational issues since this is the first time they've served brunch rather than dinner, he says. All of our drinks will be on the house, and would we care to order another round?

Ten minutes later, the food arrives. But unfortunately for my two grown children, it's not the French toast stuffed with Grand Marnier-spiked cream cheese they had ordered. This French toast is flat and puny—definitely not stuffed. But famished after waiting for more than an hour, they dig in anyway. I flag down our waitress, who returns to our table sheepishly, and before I can open my mouth, she apologizes, saying the French toast my kids originally ordered is almost done, that this pale imitation is meant to tide them over until the real dish is ready.

Thirty seconds later, and here come the waitress and the host, each bearing a plate of the stuffed French toast, each of them apologizing again and offering to make amends. We smile politely and tell them we're just fine. And for the most part, we are—the food which has finally arrived is truly delicious and attractively arranged on our plates. And the environment is still lovely.

As we're finishing our last bites, the host and waitress reappear, only this time, they are carrying between them a huge white porcelain platter on which is artfully arranged a sampling of every dessert offered by the restaurant—six in all, enormous portions. The host again apologizes for the delay in delivering our food, and announces that, like the drinks, my children's breakfasts (all four French toast entrees) as well as the desserts are compliments of the house.

Minutes later, when it's clear that we can't possibly finish the lovely desserts before us, the host whisks away the platter, returning with our sweet leftovers carefully boxed to take home. "And I noticed that you especially enjoyed the sweet rolls which preceded breakfast, so I've included a few more in the box for you," he says as he puts the pretty package on our table.

On the way home, I ask my children, "Would you go back to that restaurant, which clearly wasn't perfect, and not nearly the successful total experience we had hoped for?" "Yes," they both immediately said, with my daughter offering the following: "You know, they made some mistakes, but at least they tried to make up for them. And I really liked the food and the place. I'd give them another chance."

This was not a perfect experience by any means. But it was clear that our experience as guests was important to this restaurant, even if this time, they couldn't completely deliver on the positive perception with which we began the experience. However, since most of the touchpoints—our initial perception, the place, the people, and the product—were in alignment, we could forgive the service disconnect and give them another chance to earn our business. And we did so because they so genuinely seemed to feel badly—even embarrassed—about their inability to deliver, and tried so hard to make up for it.

For any leader, gaps can be frightening. It feels as though a slip could expose you and your enterprise for being a well-meaning but fraudulent failure. If you're just starting on your journey to making your enterprise real, you might feel that this effort is too large and all-encompassing to completely capture your ideal experience delivery in a way that no gap gets overlooked. And so you might think you would be setting up yourself and your stakeholders for a disappointing failure.

Not to worry. There is a system to launching or relaunching your enterprise in such a way that you'll design exactly the authentic enterprise of your vision. In the next chapter, we'll get started with an overview of that process, which we call *total experience design*.

Chapter 3

WHAT IS TOTAL EXPERIENCE DESIGN?

The purpose of life, after all, is to live it, to taste experience to the utmost,
to reach out eagerly and without fear for newer and richer experiences.

Eleanor Roosevelt

It's a fair bet to say that whenever a new enterprise is conceived, it is usually defined by at least one compelling idea. Maybe it's a new product. Or an innovative service. Or the kind of people you want to serve. And then you flesh out that idea one piece at a time, until a full picture is laid out either in your head, on paper, or in a computer file. You start talking about it to your friends, colleagues, vendors, associates, maybe even investors, and ideas begin to emerge with each additional conversation.

Eventually you'll have to start putting those ideas together to really bring your original stroke of brilliance into reality. This is where design begins. In a traditional design process, you're addressing all the choices as separate entities. What will your logo be like? Hire a graphic designer. Where will your office be located? Hire a real estate agent. What will your product be? Hire a business consultant. How will you get the word out? Find yourself a marketing guru. Need a Web site? Of course you do. Hire a webmaster. With each separate question, you work with a separate team of experts to help you sort out your options. This approach is time-consuming and expensive. Because you will probably have to talk to numerous candidates for each hiring decision, you have to repeat yourself multiple times—each translation slightly different from the last, giving each team a chance to get your vision wrong in their own heads. At the end of the day, you have multiple versions of your idea as expressed in logo, business plan, address, customer base, job applicants, signage, and so on. This approach takes longer to get to your ideal outcome, and chances are excellent that you'll have to redo certain pieces until you get it right.

However, there is another process that you can use to create the authentic differentiation that will set you apart in the marketplace, making it impossible for your competition to successfully imitate you. This is what I call *total experience design.* With total experience design, you are creating an authentic vision for your future, and addressing all the aspects of it at once in a holistic and integrated fashion. You focus on designing the ultimate experiences your stakeholders will be expecting from your enterprise, and you fill in the details, holding the same ultimate picture in your mind and in the minds of your team who will help you bring this image to life. Total experience design starts with your authentic, shared vision, and with your team you intentionally design, in an integrated fashion, all the essential components of your enterprise from the very start.

Hence, total experience design always has these four guiding concepts:

- *The design is authentic:* The vision is rooted in a solid belief in a promise to all of your stakeholders.
- *The design is based on a vision shared by the entire team:* All the participants on the design team—even including the stakeholders themselves—hold the same outcome in their minds.
- *The design is intentional:* Nothing is left to chance. All choices pertaining to the new enterprise are made specifically in concert with the commitment to the authentic vision.
- *The design is integrated:* When the four key components of any enterprise—*Perception, People, Products and Services,* and *Place*—work together, the whole becomes significantly more powerful than the parts. These components comprise the 4Ps; the framework that governs total experience design.

In this chapter we'll look at total experience design and describe how, based upon an authentic vision, the 4P framework can help your organization tell a unique story of who it is and what it wants to mean to your community of stakeholders. First, let's start with an example of a small, local coffee shop with aspirations of providing its local community with an experience that a larger chain couldn't.

In 2001, Mark and Connie Peppel decided that they wanted to design the prototype for their vision of a chain of upscale coffee shops—Four Seasons Coffee. Their vision was to provide a high-end experience for their customers that included exceptional products and services; knowledgeable, personable staff; a welcoming, high-quality environment; as well as ongoing education for their target market: people who are passionate about coffee. They also knew the importance of differentiating their establishment from other coffee shops in their area—not the least of which is Starbucks.

"Our vision is to offer a quality product in a quality environment with quality service, and to educate the public on the nuances of coffee," says Connie Peppel. "Experience the flavor" is their tagline. "Flavor is what it's all about," she says.

Located in Brookfield, a posh, high-quality suburb of Milwaukee, and in keeping with their vision of providing exceptional quality, the 1,700-square-foot shop features top-quality materials and appointments throughout. These include cherry wood trim, porcelain cups and saucers, and free Wi-Fi (a very popular attraction among students and business customers). A cozy lounge area provides relaxed comfort with overstuffed chairs adjacent to a fireplace. And a children's activity station is strategically placed away from the adults.

Baked goods are fresh every morning, orange juice is freshly squeezed, and coffee is brewed at least every hour. In addition to the expected cinnamon rolls, Four Seasons Coffee offers chocolate-covered macaroons made for them in Chicago and traditional black-and-white cookies from New York. Other menu items include high-quality sandwiches, healthy salads, yogurt parfaits, biscotti from Italy, box lunches, and corporate gifts. It's a nice place to grab a cup of coffee and relax for a while, yes. But what makes this experience special is Connie's vision to cater to coffee connoisseurs with superior coffee, great ambience, and expert information about what they're drinking with the intention of making her customers more knowledgeable about their passion—in other words, what the Peppels have identified as a *total coffee experience.*

It's easy to see how the total coffee experience might manifest itself in the way their customers experience Four Seasons Coffee. But that's only part of the story. How does the total coffee experience actually show up in the way the Peppels make their choices in the manner in which they do business?

Typically, when one would think of design around the total coffee experience, it would be normal to assume that we are talking about the aesthetic choices that would become integrated throughout the shop: the company logo; employee uniforms; product selection; signage; menu board; letterhead and business cards; gift card design; and all paper goods, right down to the *coffee cozy* (that sleeve that slips onto paper cups to protect customers from the heat of the coffee). But the total coffee experience vision also drives decisions around the people the Peppels hire, and the operational protocols for checkout, maintenance, and trash handling. Even the decision about which coffee bean vendor they use became a moment of truth for them in terms of just how committed they were to their vision. In selecting their coffee supplier, the Peppels narrowed their choices down to two: one located in Chicago, and the other in Milwaukee.

The couple was leaning toward using the local supplier, feeling more comfortable with its proximity to their shop. But in keeping with their vision, the Peppels asked themselves, "Which vendor has the best, highest quality product to meet our desired customer experience?" The Chicago supplier, with a higher quality and better tasting product, won hands down. True to their vision, they selected the more expensive, top-quality coffee bean—along with the Chicago supplier—and passed up the more affordable, local supplier.

The Peppels used their 4P framework to weigh all their decisions, which resulted in their coming up with some very frugal and creative solutions to business challenges for which larger companies typically have a healthy budget. Naturally, for instance, a small business such as Four Seasons Coffee doesn't have the kind of marketing firepower or paid marketing staff as does a company such as Starbucks to drive a specific *perception* of its business. So it was crucial that the Peppels focus their limited time and resources on those activities that are consistent with and will most effectively and authentically express and build their brand.

As part of the branding strategy, and consistent with its upscale vision, Four Seasons Coffee positioned itself as part of the local community with its strong quality of life, and as a strong supporter of the arts. The Sharon Lynne Wilson Center for the Arts, a local venue for performing arts presentations, festivals, arts education, family programs, community events, and private parties, was the perfect fit for a marketing partnership. So Four Seasons Coffee developed a unique Wilson Center blend of coffee, which the center serves at its events. In turn, Four Seasons Coffee donates 10 percent of its profits to the center.

And with a nod toward engaging in the surrounding community, Four Seasons Coffee also works with the local office of the American Cancer Society, placing its coffees and teas in their offices and at their special events.

Similarly, in keeping with its high-end image, Four Seasons Coffee partners with a local Lexus dealer and a nearby day spa. In return for a good deal on coffee for its customers, both venues provide Four Seasons Coffee brand signage near their coffee service areas.

The Four Seasons Coffee shop itself also serves as a meeting place for small groups where learning is the focus, such as a knitting club, a book club, and a local chapter of l'Alliance Française (an international organization that promotes French language and culture). The Peppels had numerous choices for partnerships to market their new venture, but they chose those that were most in keeping with their authentic vision for high quality. All of the activities they selected are in keeping with the shop's commitment to be a strong local presence in the community, both aligning itself with charities it can be proud of and supporting the community's high quality of life.

Customers increase their coffee knowledge at the Four Seasons Coffee Bar. *Photo by Edward J. Purcell, EPAP, Ltd.*

Because customer education and learning about coffee emerged as a major driver for growing the business, and one which would differentiate the shop from the plethora of coffee shops springing up throughout the country, the Peppels decided that a coffee tasting bar should be included in the store design (separated from the normal floor traffic). In addition to catering to small groups of customers, coffee tasting sessions are offered periodically for groups of up to 40 people, followed by discounted pricing on purchases. By understanding their customers' palate for various foods and chocolates, well-trained and personable employees guide customers toward the types of coffee they're likely to appreciate. People who like spicy food, for example, tend to prefer full-bodied coffee. A customer who says, "I'm having guests for a lamb dinner and I'm wondering what kind of coffee would be best to complement the meal," can expect knowledgeable guidance.

The total coffee experience incorporates numerous peripheral activities: relaxing and socializing, reading the morning paper, surfing the Internet, studying or working, enjoying good food, and trying different coffee flavors. Though the Peppels have these bases covered, there's also more than enough to add to the total coffee experience—based upon the Peppels' creativity and authentic vision—to keep their business fresh, inviting, and *differentiated from their competitors.*

What is the value of designing a total experience? Having an authentic vision out of which come critical decision-making drivers will help you to more quickly and easily make critical choices. You will integrate all aspects of your organization from the very beginning, consistent with your ultimate vision for your enterprise. It's not just about creating an attractive space. It's about creating a living, integrated world that welcomes all your stakeholders, and where they can depend on all the details ringing true consistently.

DESIGNING THE TOTAL EXPERIENCE

You can design the total experience down to the smallest detail, and for every moment of customer or employee interaction. It is at this point where the 4Ps of total experience become critical touchpoints for integrated, total experience design.

Perception

Your vision for your enterprise is communicated both directly and indirectly to your stakeholders, creating a perception about the organization in the minds of your customers, employees, and prospects. This helps to determine how your various stakeholders feel about you, as well as helps you attract the right stakeholders in the first place. Businesses directly communicate this vision through marketing methods such as advertising, special events, direct mail campaigns, social media, and public/community relations activities designed to communicate what the business or organization offers and how the offering is made.

When the intended perception of your organization is consistent with your stakeholders' real world experience of the organization, *brand balance* occurs, and customer loyalty is created and strengthened at every positive interaction. However, when the promise or perception is not backed up with the actual experience, *brand disconnect* occurs. And then the opportunity for differentiation and creating customer loyalty is lost, and most likely lost for good, along with the customer.

Clearly, disconnects between the perception and the reality of the customer experience can hurt the bottom line of any business. Losing existing customers is bad business economics. It is far more costly to acquire a new customer than it is to simply retain an existing customer. Moreover, enhancing the perception of a company, as long as it's validated by the customer experience, can reduce customer defections—and may even bolster the company's stock value. In fact, states *BusinessWeek,* "a company's reputation for being able to deliver growth, attract top talent, and avoid ethical mishaps can account for much of the 30–70 percent gap between the book value of most companies and their market capitalizations."[1]

People

Is the *best* product or service offering enough to trump uninspired or poor service by the people who work for you? Increasingly these days, the answer is no. It used to be that customers would put up with poor service, if they knew they were getting the best in terms of the product.

Think about your own experiences—the top healthcare specialist with a terrible bedside manner or an insufferably indifferent waiter at the finest restaurant in town. You probably have no trouble coming up with a time when your expectations for a high-quality experience were disappointed by lackluster or even hostile service. It's not enough to offer the best product to clients, as products become better and more competitive (faster, stronger, cheaper). How the best is delivered is equally—if not more—important to today's sophisticated and selective client.

The people side of any business or organization is the most difficult part of any experience to get right. However, done right, it can be the single most important differentiating factor in a competitive landscape. These days, consumers have more choices than ever as to how to spend their time and money. And putting up with lousy service or a bad bedside manner isn't as acceptable as it once may have been, when good physicians or well-trained waiters were in shorter supply, or consumers did not have a great way of finding them (e.g., via the Internet) or get to them in our increasingly mobile society. For consumers who base their decisions on price, it may not matter so much how the business serves up its offering, as long as the offering is cheap. But for those consumers with more disposable income, how they are treated or served can be a key differentiator that is highly valued by a highly desirable target market.

Products and Services

Another step toward brand balance occurs when the experience of a product or service offering is consistent with the perception of the organization.

Who hasn't experienced disappointment when an actual product or service didn't live up to its advertising? Not every product must be Grade A, top quality, solid gold. It just has to be what your company says it is.

It must also align with the purported authentic vision and values of the organization. A hospital, for instance, wouldn't sell cigarettes. The President's Council on Physical Fitness would be ill-advised to raise money through a bake sale. Those are blatant brand disconnects, certainly. Some are more subtle, of course. (The Fresh Eyes Audit™ and Experience Audit described in Chapter 5 are tools that will help you to catch potential disconnects that are disrupting your prospects for success even now.)

Place

The final element in the manifestation of a differentiating total experience is the environment that supports and enhances the perception, the product/service offering, and the people making the product or delivering the service. Four Seasons Coffee is about providing not just coffee to their clients, but also education about coffee. So, of course, a coffee-tasting bar, where coffee *lessons* can take place, was a natural choice in the design of the environment.

The integration of the 4Ps provides the basis for creating total experiences that differentiate an organization. To bring your vision to life and achieve differentiation in your marketplace, you must attend to each of the critical elements of the total experience. You must also have a definitive design process that is thoughtfully planned and holistic enough to define and create total experiences where all 4Ps come together and deliver precisely the experience you want all of your stakeholders to enjoy.

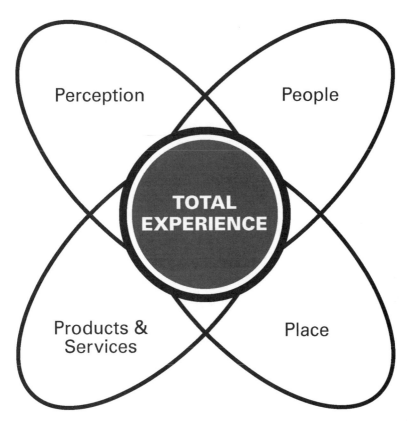

4P Model™

From the very beginning, Paul Berlin of Sabor, a Brazilian *churrascaria,* realized the need for a clearly defined vision as the basis for the perceptual, operational, and physical design of his new restaurant. The *churrascaria* is a steakhouse concept that started in Brazil in the 1980s, but its origins date back more than three centuries to the life of *gauchos* (South American cowboys) driving cattle and cooking their food fireside-style on the plains of South America.

At Sabor, diners pay a fixed price for an all-you-can-eat meal. *Gauchos* arrive tableside with knives and a skewer on which is speared a selection of fire-roasted cuts of meat offered to customers until they are well-satisfied. At Sabor, diners signal the roaming *gauchos* with a color-coded disk at each place setting: green for "Bring more!" and red for "Stop! I've had enough for now."

Berlin's vision was to be the premier steakhouse in Milwaukee, where his guests would be entertained while being treated to impeccable service and high-quality food, resulting in a multisensory experience as pleasing to the senses as it is to the palate.

In addition, the idea of providing an experience that was simple, yet elegant, was a part of Sabor's development from the beginning. "Our branding began with simplicity for our guests. We knew we had to come up with a short name or one that could be easily shortened," said Berlin. "We're officially 'Sabor Brazilian Churrascaria,' but our guests call us 'Sabor,' which is Portuguese for flavor."

Because Berlin decided to introduce his customers to an authentic Brazilian steakhouse tradition, he used the authentic vocabulary to do so. Thus, the official name signals to customers that this is something new and different. But the shortened version of the original name is much simpler and easier for customers to understand, to remember, and certainly to pronounce.

Berlin invested a year in developing the total experience design to support his vision, making sure all 4Ps were covered. Key Perception issues, developed and addressed, revolved around brand essence, promise and image, all advertising, Web site and marketing materials (including brochures for the table, which describe in detail the different grilled meat and chicken options being served). The People element of the experience involved determining what kinds of people to hire, the design of staff uniforms, training, employee protocols, and recruiting. Products and Services issues included determining the choice of food and wine options, as well as the design of the kitchen and dining room layout and development of protocols to determine how the total experience would be delivered from an operational point of view. The selection of tableware and linens, flowers, the choice of background music—even what type of after-dinner mints should be offered at the hostess stand—came under the Products and Services consideration. And Place, as one would expect, addressed elements such as exterior and interior design, color, signage, lighting, furniture, fixtures, flooring, and artwork.

An overriding question was how Berlin could make Sabor different from its competition. A competition audit (which we'll discuss in greater detail in Chapter 5) revealed that *churrascaria* restaurants in the United States had captured the *gaucho* theme but usually translated the experience into a kind of cattle drive—"get 'em in and get 'em out"—rather than offering up the pleasure of dining according to time-honored Brazilian traditions.

Through the competition audit, Berlin was able to identify a very commercial vibe at other Brazilian steakhouses that was not at all based on the authentic experience of the *gaucho* on which the whole *churrascaria* concept was originally based. Berlin decided that the Sabor experience would be much simpler and more elegant than its competition, believing that if the focus was on the food and the experience, the brand would sell itself. Additionally, understanding that the market in which the restaurant was located trended in the direction of more low-key, comfortable, unassuming evenings, this approach would provide his patrons with the special, personal evening that they wanted. Guests would feel comfortable coming as they were—evening gowns to blue jeans—and feel that they could linger over dinner as long as they chose to.

During the course of the year, Berlin made manifest his vision by identifying the essential characteristics—or *Project Drivers,* which I describe in more detail in Chapter 6—that would influence his business decisions from that point forward and differentiate his *churrascaria* from that of his competition:

- Hiring the best people. Training, motivating, and encouraging them, and thereby retaining the friendliest, most efficient staff.
- Creating a unique, innovative, entertaining, Brazilian-style atmosphere that will differentiate us from the competition.
- Executing our primary goal to serve nothing but the highest quality food with impeccable service in a clean, lively, and exciting environment. We must deliver on this pledge 100 percent of the time, without exception.
- Controlling costs at all times, in all areas.
- Creating a *wow!* environment.

Berlin and his design team chose the four natural elements of earth, air, fire, and water as the unifying elements through which these essential drivers would be made manifest in both subtle and direct ways. Starting at the front entry, the distinctive Sabor logo above the door communicates activity, motion, and energy. The bronze door handle resembles a lariat, the basic tool used by *gauchos* to drive cattle.

Inside the vestibule, a cascading water feature provides the next *wow!,* followed by a distinctive, two-story, 2,500-bottle wine cellar. An adjacent two-story coatroom is enclosed behind rich, mahogany panels, freeing up floor space for tables; the restaurant provides total seating for up to 200 guests.

Earth is represented by dramatic wood beams throughout the space and the warm, natural earth tones used throughout the restaurant. Three dining rooms with high ceilings provide a spacious, airy feeling, which is enhanced by ethereal overhead lighting fixtures in the main dining room which manifest the element of Air. When the air vents are engaged, the current causes the lights to move ever so slightly. Fire not only is expressed most obviously in the grill, but also is captured in the red walls that contrast with the Cream City brick, a naturally light-colored brick that is manufactured from soil native to the area.

"If you walk into a building that's dark and filled with unhappy people, it's very depressing . . . it's about quiet. We're not that. We're about fun and energy," says Berlin. "The atmosphere of a restaurant is dictated by two things: design and people. And they have to work together perfectly. We feel we offer a service level that's unmatched." The restaurant opened in 2006 to rave reviews, and continues to attract new customers as it serves a growing base of repeat guests.

Another way Berlin helps ensure a successful and differentiated experience in the highly competitive world of food service is by focusing on the People side of the Sabor experience—the quality of his wait staff. That doesn't have to involve a complex hiring regimen—it's actually pretty simple, says Berlin. The three top priorities in all of his employment interviews are: Is this a happy person, and does it show? Is this a nice person? Does this person smile?

Berlin says he can train his staff for everything else. But he can't make them happy, pleasant, or helpful people, nor can he force them to smile. But if they already possess those characteristics, he can be satisfied that they will take proper care of the guests in his restaurant. Berlin avoids the term *customers*. "They're guests in my home," he says.

Berlin sets a good example as the embodiment of his vision for the Sabor experience. He is obviously a happy person himself, punctuating his conversation with jovial laughter and an ever-present smile. He enjoys the pleasures of good food and dining, and his enjoyment is contagious.

"We need to make the atmosphere comfortable and relaxing for our guests. If we start them out right, then they're going to notice those big smiles on our servers' faces. With a high level of service from pleasant, helpful people, guests are even apt to overlook a missing fork at the table or other minor faux pas," Berlin says.

Although Berlin focuses on the quality of the wait staff, he is equally focused on the myriad details that make up what Pine and Gilmore call the *eatertainment* experience (where good food + good ambiance = great entertainment).[2] From the local charm of the building's Cream City brick construction to the simple elegance of the waiters' uniforms, from the background music to the design and functionality of the tableware, there isn't a brand touchpoint that escapes his attention.

Authentic brand differentiation comes across in everything, most especially in the details. The logo at Sabor, for instance. In other Brazilian steakhouses, the logo is plastered on everything. At Sabor, where comfort, simplicity, and elegance are the focus, the simple black jackets worn by the valets have a small Sabor logo on the sleeve of the jacket, which is what most customers see as the valet opens the door to their car or to the restaurant. And the typically overdone, multilayered, logo-plastered *gaucho* uniform worn by Sabor's competitors is simplified. For the *gauchos* at Sabor, the uniform includes simple, nicely tailored blue shirts (playing off the water element in nature) and black slacks.

This attention to detail extends to tableware, from the use of natural materials in the interior design to the copper chargers on each table. Food serves

Sabor serves up a multisensory Brazilian steakhouse experience. *Photo © Todd Dacquisto.*

as the star of the show, so basic white table linens and flatware with clean, simple lines were selected. The china is also a basic white, serving as a backdrop for the colorful food. Riedel stemware, with its elegant, understated lines, is the preferred crystal of serious wine drinkers, reinforcing the simple elegance of the experience. Guests at Sabor have reported that the total experience does indeed feel warm and welcoming, with a level of simple, elegant sophistication that is comfortable and appreciated.

With a restaurant as highly designed as Sabor, it's fairly easy to see how brand touchpoints can be made physically manifest in the food and the place. It's obvious that the people or wait staff in a restaurant should walk and talk the restaurant's brand. And if the perception of the eatery isn't in keeping with the products, the service, the people, and the place, then the restaurant's marketing efforts are going to miss their mark. Careful design and integration of

Touchpoints

Perception
Logo
Name
Web Site
Brochures
Newsletters & Mailings
Graphics
Advertisements
Special Events
Marketing & PR
Letterhead
Business Cards
Altruistic/Community Involvement

People
Staff Training & Development
Knowledge
Helpfulness
Courtesy
Empowerment
Management
Hospitality
Uniforms
Nametags

Products & Services
Amenities
Logistics
Operations
Wait Times
Hours of Operation
Accessibility
Quality of Service
Product Placement
Product Packaging
Food and Beverage

Place
Adjacencies
Artwork/Graphics
Furniture & Fixtures
Lighting
Location
Music/Sound System
Parking
Signage & Wayfinding
Style, Colors
Views
Ambience
Noise, Cleanliness
Technology
Landscape

Copyright © Kahler Slater, Inc.

brand touchpoints is what clearly differentiates one organization from another, no matter what the industry. And, too often, these touchpoints are overlooked and not integrated into a cohesive, authentic, and differentiating experience.

Customer experiences don't have to be left to chance, and in fact should be designed down to the smallest touchpoint. And only by doing so can the experience be replicated and leveraged for ongoing future success.

How does each of these elements currently contribute to or detract from your organization's vision? How might they be changed to more positively align with the organization's vision? Bringing your vision to life in a manner that is authentic to your organization to achieve differentiation in your marketplaces requires attending to each of the critical elements of a total experience.

Having a clear understanding of your organization's vision and future aspirations is essential to setting the stage for the total experience design process, which comprises a five-part journey. But first, it's important to know whether you and your organization are truly ready for this adventure into committing yourselves to the differentiating transformation that total experience design can bring.

Chapter 4

GO BIG OR DON'T BOTHER

I think a major act of leadership right now, call it a radical act, is to create the places and processes so people can actually learn together, using our experiences.

Margaret J. Wheatley

You are a visionary leader with big dreams for the future. You know that to achieve your goals, best your competition, and stand out in a crowded marketplace you must authentically differentiate your organization. And now you have decided to go through the rigorous process of identifying what your marketplace difference will be, and how that difference will be made manifest in all of the ways your stakeholders experience your enterprise. Your organization is facing some important changes in its immediate future. And as its leader, you are going to be the one ultimately responsible for making sure those changes take hold.

So there is one last important question for you to answer before launching into your transformational future: *are you really ready?*

You're a leader, so that means you most likely have been in your field or profession for a significant amount of time. Certainly long enough to have seen at least a couple of change initiatives crash and burn because the senior leadership wasn't really committed to going through the pain and uncertainty that come with any important change project. Are you ready to commit to a journey that doesn't yet have a clear path? Are you ready to let your team members help drive this transformation? Are you ready to relinquish control to those who share your vision, but who may have other, better, faster roads to get you to your destination? Are you ready to make a long-term commitment to this effort, knowing that this process is not about quick fixes, but rather creating change that leads to sustainable results for the long haul? Are you ready to transform your organization in such a way that there's no going back?

Transformation requires leaders who refuse to take no for an answer, who know how challenging the process will be, but who march ahead anyway, secure in the conviction that their dream can, must, and will be realized. It takes courage, as bringing anything new or different to the marketplace has its challenges, including the possibility of being ignored by a public who isn't ready for your new offering, or being challenged by investors who simply want to see a return on their money—now. Or working with a board of directors who may have their own agenda and ideas for your organization's future. But most of all, it takes a commitment to stay the course, even when those around you don't understand or, worse, don't believe in your vision for transformation.

At the same time, it takes bringing those very same people along as well, as far into the change process as you can take them without putting the transformation itself at risk. They could ultimately be your best advocates and idea generators. You need as many people as possible to come along with you, even the ones who don't agree with you at first. Why? Because if it's only visionary leadership at the table, there's a danger of never getting out of the dreaming mode. If it's only practical leadership at the table, the bar may not be set high enough because the focus might be on only what is most obviously or cost effectively achievable. However, in combination, and by recruiting and involving a highly diverse team, 1 plus 1 can equal 200. Thus, the people who lead the process actually mirror the process itself—one that uses diversity of thought and ideas to transcend old ways of thinking, creating more authentic and sustainable results than anyone could have ever imagined.

With total experience design, you are taking on a complete overhaul of the way you run your organization. This is not about incremental change. It's monumental. A successful total transformation always is monumental. But a failure can be as well, even if the result of all your efforts is what others might regard as merely boring. And that's bad. If you're reaching for total experience design, a ho-hum or business-as-usual change is a crashing disaster.

The chances for success all start with the leader—you. For this reason, it's essential to know whether you are ready for the journey. And then whether your team is ready. And, finally, whether you and your team are ready to work together.

If you decide that you're not, that's okay for now. At least you know. And it's better that you know now.

Here's how to tell.

YOU THE LEADER

You Are Willing to Leave the Present Condition Behind

Even if the present represents the manifestation of some earlier dreams of yours that have finally come true, you are willing to leave the present condition behind. Total experience design that results in organizational transformation isn't just about going in the direction of a new and wonderful vision of the future. It's also about moving away from the familiar and perhaps even comfortable experience of the present. This can be especially difficult if the present condition represents an arrival that you had worked so hard to earn. Not all that's now is outdated, dysfunctional, bad, or tired. There are many aspects to the now condition that are still completely serviceable, and maybe even still cherished within your current culture. But if these aspects and traditions don't serve the new vision of the total experiences you wish to design, you may still have to get rid of them.

This might be harder than you can imagine. The furniture in the reception area? Even if it's only a year or so old? Painful to replace, but doable. You won't be the first leader to have sunk many thousands of dollars into an aesthetic facelift, only to discover very quickly that what was really needed was a major structural or cultural overhaul. You may end up changing embedded operational traditions entirely. Or, if you're in education, asking a tenured professor to completely change the way curriculum is delivered to students. Or, if you're in medicine, requiring doctors to redesign the way they deliver healthcare so that the patient comes first. What about the people who spent long, hard years earning the privileges of seniority, only to discover that you're proposing that they turn their professional lives upside down—even to the point where they might have to acquiesce to more junior colleagues? They may not be very happy with you. But that culture overhaul may be exactly what's necessary to bring your enterprise into a differentiated future. And if that means that your leadership team loses the privileges of their seniority, you may face a tremendous amount of resistance from your higher-ranking staff who are only just now understanding that total experience design could totally redesign their personal experience of stature, success, and organizational power.

And, of course, there is your own position to consider. As the leader, you've come a long way to achieving your rank, working very hard as you made the climb. You might have suffered in a hidebound hierarchical structure over decades, knowing that eventually you will have paid your dues and "all this will be yours one day." And now, facing a total experience design overhaul, how much of *all this* will you be willing to throw out the window into the big dumpster below? Now is the time to be really clear that you know the answer to that question.

By the way, there is no right or wrong answer to that question. It's just wrong not to *know* the answer. If you pull back on your commitment part-way through the transformation because you discover that you were actually more attached to the way things are now than you had thought you were, the damage you could do will be worse than had you done nothing at all.

Are You Willing to Share the Ownership of the Change?

Because total experience design usually involves transformational cultural change, your chances of success skyrocket when you bring your entire community of stakeholders onboard as your visionary partners—even your customers. There should not be an *us-versus-them* dichotomy if you want your community to be, ultimately, a team of excited colleagues as passionate about your vision as you are. It must be a shared vision, not a fiefdom with one leader.

Again, this may sound good in theory. But in actual practice and experience, this will mean that everyone you invite to participate in the transformation process will have a voice and a say. And it's not unheard of for a senior executive to be outnumbered by the entire community who sees the same vision—although their version might be slightly askew of yours. This is not a revolt; it's collaboration. If it feels like a revolt to you, then perhaps you're not ready.

In fact, your power to affect change actually grows as you are willing to share the power with all of your stakeholders. This may or may not be a democracy, ultimately. But it is a collaborative, visionary process in which you are asking everyone to leave their present behind—a present that they might actually be quite fond of. So your best chance for a successful transformation is to give your stakeholders the opportunity to be excited about the possibilities—even though they may be as yet unknown. True, sustainable excitement is most easily achieved when they have the chance to be part of the formulating team. And for that to happen, you must be willing to share that ownership.

Can You Be Comfortable with the Ambiguity of the Iterative Process?

Total experience design can be a messy proposition. Not all changes will happen instantly and by decree. Some will have to be slowly adopted. Some will have to be modified as they are proven to be not quite right in reality—even though they looked great on the proverbial drawing board. As with every redesign or renovation, much debris results from the demolition phase. Can you tolerate the rubble and dust of the old ways as your enterprise is waiting to be swept clean before the new fixtures, fittings, practices, people, and processes arrive?

Do You Have a Track Record and Reputation for Being Faithful to Your Team?

When you ask your stakeholders to join you on this venture, you're asking them to take important risks—many of which have to do with their careers and personal, financial security. If you are asking them to rethink or perhaps throw away everything they've worked for and with for the sake of a vision that has yet to be created, they must trust you to stand by that ultimate vision even when the pressure is on to fold, compromise, or capitulate.

This is not only about watching your budget. Of course, you don't have to commit at the very outset to the most expensive or exotic choices to manifest your vision (be it a new conference room table, a new address, or hiring a star player in your industry). You can suffer pressure from a wide variety of corners: Wall Street's quarter-by-quarter expectations; clients you profoundly disagree with, but on whom you can rely to give you a project when times are tight; a sales manager who gets results but who bullies your customers and employees. Will you have what it takes to dismiss that sales manager to protect the integrity of the culture you have specifically designed with the help of all your stakeholders? Even if it means a sharp dip in revenue?

Your team is more likely to throw in their lot with yours, even if the vision isn't quite set in stone yet, if they know they can count on your commitment to see the whole process through. And that you will stand by them as they feel their own way through the resulting change.

You Have Control over Your Inner Control Freak

As the leader of your organization, your job is to be the vision champion as you take your group through the transformation process. There will be times throughout the process when the group might lose sight of what your team is working together to achieve. It will be up to you to remind and refocus your team. You have to be the one to exert control.

At the same time, you know that this is about a shared endeavor of your entire community of stakeholders. It won't be entirely successful unless everyone can experience the rewards of their shared endeavor. This transformation is a story that your entire team must create and own, not only as a group but also as individuals. So as much as it's your job to ferociously champion the vision, it's also your job to sit back and let others drive the process at times.

You Understand That Your Behaviors Model the Desired Vision, Even Now

If your total experience design incorporates a change in the way your people treat each other and your customers, start modeling those behaviors now. See how it feels to you. If you want a collaborative community of coworkers, you don't have to wait until the last layer of paint has been applied to your new walls before you start demonstrating what collaboration looks like in terms of the way you treat your people—and the way you model how you expect your people to treat each other.

YOUR TEAM

They Are Open to Possibilities

Not everyone must be on the side of change at the outset. When there is change, there will always be people who will worry that they might lose something valuable to them—their careers or their turf. However, if you have just enough people on your team who are excited about the prospects of the changes that will come about as the entire group journeys through the transformation, you will have your internal change evangelists who will champion your shared vision. And as traditional change management theory suggests, the more love and attention you shine on the people who embrace the opportunity to change for the better, and the less attention you offer to the naysayers (who aren't inclined to change based on even your most persuasive arguments anyway), the more you'll have the undecideds joining the first camp. Who wouldn't want more love and attention?

They Trust That They Won't Be Punished for Speaking Their Minds

And yet, even the resistant voices deserve to be heard without fear of retribution. These people aren't threatening the success of your initiatives, even though it might feel that way from time to time. They may ultimately become your most exuberant converts. Or they might leave. Whatever the outcome, as you and your team move through the total experience design process, they are your opportunity to demonstrate through your actions that you're dedicated to the transformation mission. And your hope is to bring everyone who is willing into the new vision.

It's not just about getting people involved so that they are more likely to own the end result. As you and your team go through the 5D (Discover, Dream, Define, Design, Deliver) Process that will be described in Part 2, silos and hierarchies should be dissolved whenever it's possible and appropriate. You will get surprising insights from people who are seeing an old problem for the first time. And when people are working shoulder-to-shoulder with coworkers who might normally be their superiors or subordinates, a respectful cross-pollination of ideas will cement working relationships that might ultimately transform as your change process continues. Diversity of thought and opinion is what drives innovation, so the more diverse the voices at the table, the better the ideas will flow, and the more creative and groundbreaking they'll be.

Your Team Clearly Sees What Their Role Is in the Total Experience Design

Everyone has a part; everyone has a stake in its success. No one is left out, even the doubters and naysayers. Even your customers, vendors, suppliers, and perhaps community leaders have a role in the transformation you seek to achieve. You have invited them to the table. And they have accepted the invitation.

MAYBE YOU'RE NOT READY FOR TOTAL EXPERIENCE DESIGN

It's hard to argue against the value of providing authentic experiences for your customers, employees, and other stakeholders. Every healthy leader naturally wants to think of himself or herself as someone committed to providing high-quality experiences for everyone associated with the organization. But creating and sustaining an authentic organization requires a rigorous, steadfast commitment to the vision. And that will take courage and single-mindedness—which can be extremely challenging when competing interests perhaps tempt you to table the discussion *for the time being*. When that happens, you lose the confidence of all your people. So it's better to know now that perhaps you're not quite ready to make that leap of commitment.

Here are some examples of how this might *not* be a good time for you or your organization to launch a total experience design project:

You Have Been with Your Organization for Less Than One Year

This might seem like the perfect time to launch a total experience design (or redesign). You're looking for a chance to make your mark on your new organization! But, in fact, this is your time to build the trust of your new community and demonstrate through your actions that you're there to serve them—not turn their world upside down. Unless you are taking over an organization that is in absolute shambles, you will be assuming leadership of people who want to be respected and recognized for the quality of work they're doing right now. By imposing a total experience design project on direct reports who are still strangers to you, you could be sending the message to them that what they've been doing all along has been all wrong. That's not the way to build a loyal following, one which you'll need to help you succeed along the way.

True, there are exceptions to this rule (as with all rules). But, overall, as you're beginning a new tenure as a leader, your first task is to build your constituency by supporting them in what they're already doing and demonstrating your commitment to fixing aspects of the business that they have identified as needing to be fixed. Build a track record of someone who follows through on promises, and you will be developing the following you'll need to see you through the major changes that will emerge from the total experience design.

You Have a Reputation for Abandoning Pet Projects

This self-knowledge pill is a bitter one, to be sure. But there's no getting past the fact that organizations waste millions of dollars and irreplaceable time by picking up flavor-of-the-month organizational theories and business ideas and then abandoning them when a new trend comes along or leaders get distracted by new flavors. Few leaders want to actually admit that they're the ones who are contributing to a short-attention-span culture. But if you think you might be one of those people who are promoting a lack of follow-through in change initiatives, you will want to build up your credibility before asking your people to sign up for this new adventure. Or you may want to team with or assign another recognized leader in your organization to work closely with you—someone with a reputation and track record for getting projects successfully across the finish line. With total experience design, you're asking your employees to put their careers on the line for the sake of this new community-generated vision. They have to count on you and/or other senior and influential leadership to be there for them during the transitional period.

You Want Your Company to Be on a *Best Employers* List

What could possibly be wrong with that? Doesn't everyone want to be known as a best employer? Maybe. But aspiring to be on a list doesn't actually make you a great employer. It's not enough to want to be on the list. To make total experience design a success, you want to be the leader of a company where people come to work inspired and excited about doing their best for a shared, defined, and authentic vision. Whether you actually make any formal list or not is entirely beside the point. It's a nice-to-have, not a must-have.

You Gain Some Comfort in Knowing That
You Can Always Fall Back on Plan B

There is no Plan B. This is it. Total experience design is going to require that you commit yourself to an extraordinary vision that is very likely one-of-a-kind in several ways. You're going to be pioneering new ideas for the way you deliver your services and the experiences your employees can count on. Some of those new approaches will undo what has been done before. Some might offend people who have a personal stake in keeping the old ways intact. You will likely run into opposition from someone somewhere from the old system. But you owe it to everyone who has followed you thus far to stay committed to Plan A.

Assuming you and your team create a total experience design that completely ignites the passion and imagination of your community, it will be worth the adventure—even the costs associated with that venture. Because you understand that the value of sustainable, authentic differentiation, which can help you secure wildly loyal clients who recommend you to others, is more than worth the costs involved to get you there.

GREAT OPPORTUNITIES FOR LAUNCHING TOTAL EXPERIENCE DESIGN

Ideally, it's simplest for any leader to launch a total experience design project at the birth of a brand-new enterprise—before you sign the lease agreement, commission your logo design, hire your first employee, even decide exactly what your product or service will be and what kinds of customers you want to attract. You have a blank slate. And you can write anything you want to on it without having to undo decisions and change entrenched minds.

Those opportunities can be seized upon by any entrepreneur, since every enterprise starts out with that blank slate. However, not every leader has the luxury of being able to grab that opportunity to design their ideal total experience approach from scratch. Most leaders assume their leadership role in mid-story in a company's unfolding history. But that doesn't mean it's too late for you to work in concert with your key stakeholders to have a profound impact on that story.

What points in that story are the most conducive to a total experience redesign? Assuming that your relationship with your key stakeholders (not just employees but everyone who has a relationship with the company) is stable and trusting, you can launch a total experience design initiative that will put your organization on a new path of achieving its best and most authentic potential. The best points to do so are major events in time that would invite anyone to reconsider the journey they're on.

A Major Anniversary

Has your enterprise been in operation for 5 years? 10 years? 25? 50? 100? Surely these milestone years provide an opportunity for both celebration and reassessment as to whether your group is making the most of its potential.

The Commission of a New Headquarters Building

This is the time when you have the chance to use your actual new address as a physical manifestation of your vision. As you go through the design process of creating a building, you can use the same choices you make around the architecture to drive questions regarding what other ways you want to manifest your vision for the company. But first, it's a good idea to make sure you know what that vision is.

A Major Shift in Your Industry or Economy

It's always better to be in front of major industry or economic changes—perhaps to even drive them, because then you are in the power position for writing the new rules. But sometimes external circumstances force changes upon you and your organization. You can still take the proactive stance of using that forward-moving momentum as energy to drive the changes you choose—as opposed to being a victim of changing circumstances. Your industry's change could be your organization's opportunity to authentically differentiate itself from its competition.

Postcrisis Recovery

Even though I recommended that you don't try to undergo a total experience design process during your first few months after assuming the leadership role, there are times when an organization truly is in shambles after a devastating event. You might not have engineered the change or crisis, but that change or crisis may force you to reengineer your organization. No one has a stake in preserving the past; and during times of crisis, people look for a hope-inspiring vision to rally their energies around and focus on. Don't rush this recovery process, of course. When you can see your people returning to a fully functioning mode, take advantage of this moment in time and engage your people in exploring the possibility of a new future—one that is exciting and inspiring.

You own the total experience design launch process. But you're not alone. The most successful initiatives universally incorporate the voices, experiences, and perspectives of everyone who holds an interest in the organization's success. As you go through the 5D Process, you'll see that some exercises might be more appropriately done by distinct departments before bringing the results to the group at-large. But overall, diversity of the people involved in bringing ideas, innovations, and opinions enrich the experience for everyone.

Just as everyone will own the success of what your group dreams of, when they own the process, they'll also own the commitment to making those dreams come true.

REENGINEERING A CREATIVITY-CONDUCIVE CULTURE MIDSTREAM

When academics and consultants study famously creative business cultures—Pixar, for example—they understandably tend to focus on organizations that were creative from Day 1. Naturally, it's instructive to study the characteristics of these cultures, especially when you're able to map the commonalities. But it can also be a little demoralizing for leaders of established companies and cultures. How can anyone possibly turn around a creative culture that's already in full swing—with its own traditions, mores, hierarchies, habits, and expectations?

It can be done. At Kahler Slater, a design firm that's more than a century old, we turned our culture completely on its head just as it was turning 90 years old. There is almost always some kind of major change that an organization faces or needs to respond to that prompts it to design a drastic transformation. In Kahler Slater's case, it was the pending retirement of the firm's two owners, Thomas "Mac" Slater and David Kahler. The prospect of losing the two principals whose names were quite literally on the door gave us the opportunity to examine who we wanted to be in the new iteration of Kahler Slater. Additionally, a move to a new headquarters office, along with the parallel opportunity to explore new ways of working and serving our clients, also served as a catalyst for our own transformation. We didn't start out transforming our culture to be specifically supportive of the creatives we had on staff. But as the events unfolded, that's exactly what we ended up doing.

One of the initial phases of our new transformation was to determine what our marketplace wanted from architecture and design firms. The answer: experts. Our clients and potential clients said that they would choose architects who were experts in their particular areas (e.g., higher education, health care, and so forth) over generalists—no matter how excellent those generalists might be. And as our clients told us that they highly valued expertise, they also indicated that they were willing to pay more for experts than for generalists as well. At that point, Kahler Slater was made up primarily of a community of highly talented generalists.

On the theory that expertise is a by-product of passion, we asked all the members of our staff (not just the architects), "What are you passionate about? Is there a market in which you are already an expert or in which you want to be an expert? Is there a new service offering that you'd like to bring to market as an expert that you believe is wanted or needed by our clients and/or potential clients?" We asked our internally focused operations staff—marketing, finance, etc.—what expertise they could deliver to *their* clients—the Kahler Slater staff whom they supported. Along with those questions, we also wanted to know if staff would be willing to take leadership roles in pursuing markets or delivering new services in those areas. Or were they more comfortable contributing to building these specialty areas or new service offerings as team members rather than team leaders?

We decided that we wanted to grow Kahler Slater by growing individual business units established around these identified passions. We no longer just wanted to be a company of terrific generalists. We wanted to grow teams of experts organized around the areas of their passions, becoming experts in their chosen fields, learning from one another and growing their business units, and consequently, Kahler Slater. So we needed individuals who were not only passionate about their chosen areas of interest, but who also were ready to step up as leaders, entrepreneurs, and market drivers.

With this one change, Kahler Slater transformed itself from being a single enterprise, with a very senior management committee of only two people who made all the major decisions, to a collection today of a dozen business and operational units, each one making its own management and development decisions. At that time, we still had the management committee in place, but its job became primarily to support and guide the individual business and operational units toward achieving our overall firm vision, the development of which occurred in conjunction with our drive to become experts.

We also made sure that our team leaders knew that they could take or leave whatever perspectives and suggestions the management committee might have to offer them, as long as their strategies and tactics were in keeping with the overall firm vision. Ultimately, we wanted everyone within Kahler Slater to think and act like an owner of the firm, with team leaders making the essential decisions about what clients to serve and projects to pursue and how they would allocate their resources to grow their pieces of the Kahler Slater business.

We also understood that as teams of diverse creatives, each team was going to achieve its goals in its own unique way. To *over manage* this process would have killed it from the very beginning. Executive leadership of the firm knew enough at that point to guide the development of a clear Vision Statement, get the right people in the right places to execute on the vision, and to support their efforts. Many times, this meant to simply get the heck out of their way.

Over time, we collectively created our mission to grow highly creative individual contributors into teams of cooperative, collaborative talent, each team following a shared vision that was both unique to the team itself and deeply woven into Kahler Slater's vision for the firm overall. At the same time, the teams had projects in which they were creating transformations for their clients. Without proper handling, this highly charged journey of transformation and even (at times) ambiguity and uncertainty could have exploded in our faces, especially if we fell back on old ways of managing our people (which happened occasionally, to be candid). But the corrections, which were swift, came in the form of staff who tapped us on our collective shoulders, pointed to the Core Beliefs and Values section of our Vision Statement, and reminded us that our old, controlling behaviors were not in keeping with our new vision. Change wasn't just for our staff. It was something which we executive leaders needed to embrace on a daily basis as well.

The key to our own transformation was keeping in mind that we weren't managing creativity, we were managing *for* creativity.[1] And we discovered that, even though our core business was in fact a creative one, *any* business transformation is a creative endeavor. And the keystones of our own transformation can be used to build a creative transformation in any kind of organization, in any kind of industry or market.

We Infuse Diversity into Every Team and Project

Those who study natural systems have long known that the more diverse an ecosystem is, the stronger and more resilient it is to change and competition. Proponents of cultural diversity—especially inside businesses—successfully make their case that organizations with a diverse employee population are best equipped to serve a wider marketplace with more relevant products and services.

We discovered through our own experience and the experiences of our clients that teams tasked with transformation are also strengthened by the diversity of their team members. Conventional architectural and design firms are usually organized in a fairly hierarchical manner, with senior designers at the top of the pyramid directing the efforts of more junior staff below. At Kahler Slater, the business unit model has it that teams include architects and interior designers who are experts in understanding and addressing the specific needs of their marketplace, as well as staff and/or affiliates who are experts in marketing, branding, graphics, environmental and behavioral research, accounting, technology, process improvement, change management, facilitation, organizational development, and so on. And all of these experts are encouraged to contribute their unique perspectives and ideas to the mix of brainstorming and idea generation and execution. We also encourage cross-fertilization of the teams, knowing that breakthrough innovation is most likely to occur by breaking down silos. For instance, members of our health care team will invite members from the hospitality team to contribute ideas to the health care team's work when it's engaged in a project in which a hospital wants to be more patient-focused, warm, and welcoming—similar to what you might find at a high-end hotel or spa.

We Don't Take *Straight-to-DVD* Projects

During Pixar's beginnings, an early relationship with Disney caused the highly visionary group of creatives to consider Disney's suggestion that they create spin-offs of their successful, original feature movies, such as *Toy Story*. Disney had found this model to be a cash cow, but there was a high price to be paid for this particular cow. The assumption was that these spin-offs would be done at a lower cost, resulting in a lesser-quality product that would go straight to DVD, leveraging the popularity of the original feature movie but not actually surpassing or even meeting the high quality of the original. These programs couldn't even be called sequels because they were never intended to do much more than keep the story alive, keep the audiences interested in the "further adventures of . . ." and keep spitting out revenue. Pixar thought it over, and decided pretty quickly that this wasn't the model it wanted to follow. Instead, it continued to focus on producing a succession of high-quality, hit movies that sparkle from the fresh excitement of their creators who are jazzed to be working on a new adventure—not a further adventure, a *spin-off,* of something they had already done. Each project is expected to be top drawer, not *straight to DVD.*[2]

Likewise, Kahler Slater teams seek out relationships and projects around which they can truly rally their passions. Team leaders actively look for opportunities to work with visionary, altruistic clients who aren't interested in the status quo, but who are aching to bring new, authentic, and highly differentiating experiences to their respective markets. We don't just chase after any money-making possibility. We pass on many projects that don't fit our criteria. Best still, our teams know that they will have full support of Kahler Slater's owners when they do take a pass on a project. If one of the *3EOs*— instead of having just one CEO, as companies typically do, we have three, so we call ourselves 3EOs—were to even suggest that a team take on a project (much less a project they didn't want to do), the team members would look at us as if we had lost our minds, which leads us to the next keystone of managing for creativity.

The Kahler Slater Executive Team Released Control and Power over the Company

To Mac Slater's and David Kahler's credit, they began relinquishing control as they approached retirement. They had already identified their two heirs apparent, and soon I was invited to join as the third 3EO. But our job is not to tell the Kahler Slater creatives what to do. Our job is to support them in doing what they do best. We also have to make the tough decisions necessary to keep the company moving forward into the future as a single organization, but what we do is in the spirit of supporting all the talent so that they can bring the company into that future as an extraordinary organization.

It took a while for our staff to trust this shift of power. But we were committed to this new approach. And eventually everyone understood that the direction of the company was in their hands now. And they are truly partners in the design of Kahler Slater as an enterprise with a future that excites everyone.

Likewise, Kahler Slater employees have enormous autonomy. Notice that I didn't say, "We gave them autonomy." That would imply that someone inside Kahler Slater has the power to take it back. No one has that kind of power. No one has the power or role to look over anyone's shoulder to make sure they're doing their jobs. We screen very carefully during the hiring process, so by the time we bring people onboard, we're confident that they are self-motivated to be responsible for their work. We have a 45-hour workweek, and our people can budget those 45 hours however it makes the most sense to them. As long as client obligations are fulfilled, the team leaders know what's going on, and collaboration with other staff members is a regular occurrence, individuals arrange their days pretty much as they see fit. This not only releases their creativity and confidence to do their best work, but it also releases them to make sure their work lives and personal lives are in balance, which is one of our criteria for being offered formal legal ownership in the firm. We've found that potential owners (associate principals and principals) who aren't living balanced personal and professional lives are on their way to burnout, which doesn't serve them, their families, their clients, or our enterprise well.

We Have Measurements of Success

Through the years we have determined that a healthy culture that is conducive to creativity must have certain characteristics—rules of composition, so to speak—that help Kahler Slater employees fully engage their unique talents, continue to grow as individuals, and contribute to Kahler Slater's vitality. We use them as part of our annual review and professional development process, but their main value is to help guide a creative culture throughout the year. We call this our *Balanced Scorecard,* based in part on a performance measurement framework originated by Drs. Robert Kaplan (Harvard Business School) and David Norton.

Kahler Slater staff are assessed on a 1-2-3 basis, with 3 meaning that the staff member is "Going above and beyond (expectations) in this area." Because of our confidence in our screening process, we assume that everyone's baseline performance is at least a 2, that they are "Doing a good job in the general expectations" of their role. If an employee's evaluation suggests at any time that he or she is a 1, "Needs improvement in the area," the team leader will work with that staff member to develop an action plan to get them back on track. Employees who are consistently assessed as 3s highly correlate with those who become recognized as firm leaders—associates, associate principals, principals, vice presidents, and 3EOs.

Our Balanced Scorecard is as follows:

1. I consistently demonstrate the Kahler Slater Core Beliefs and Values of Relationships/Trust, Respectful Collaboration, Passion/Creativity, Integrity, and Openness.
2. I am succeeding in my current responsibilities and at my responsibility level.
3. I am actively engaged with the enterprise to share/develop cool design ideas, process ideas, and technology ideas.
4. I have happy and satisfied clients.
5. I contribute to my team being juiced and stoked.
6. I contribute toward meeting team revenue goals and/or controlling team or firm expenses.

We Consider Everyone a Contributor to Kahler Slater's Creative Culture

We count on all Kahler Slater employees to identify with the creative vision of the firm. So we require that everyone take part in eight to ten hours of creative activities per year, over and above that which happens naturally as they engage with their clients on projects. Some Kahler Slater employees, such as the architects, need little to no encouragement to live a more creative life. Others, such as administrative staff, might not feel welcome to participate in creative activities in other firms. But our creative culture brings everyone under one creative umbrella. And so, administrative or other operations staff are encouraged to attend client creative workshops (even for projects that they may not necessarily be officially a part of). Or they take part in our *creativity firedrills,* which occur several times a year and during which people are encouraged—but not required—to share with the rest of the staff what they're working on. Other creativity activities include our *midweek movie madness,* when we show videos during lunch about a wide range of creativity-related ideas and projects. We also conduct numerous and ongoing design charettes, in which designers can explore ideas about the projects they're working on, not only with their own teams, but also with members of other teams who are encouraged to share their unique and fresh perspectives.

In our culture, *no one individual is a creative superstar.* In conventional design and architecture firms, the perception is that much of the work and renown revolves around the name and charisma of just a few people. In Kahler Slater's earlier years, that would have been David Kahler, who was the established name in architecture back in his day. However, as even David himself would tell you, as talented a designer as he was and is, design is truly a team sport. The most innovative solutions rarely, if ever, spring full-blown from the mind of a single creator. Even Thomas Edison, the most creative of inventors, surrounded himself with a team as curious and risk-taking as he was. And yet, when David Kahler retired, those who watched Kahler Slater from afar worried that his departure might signal the end of the firm.

Because his retirement was coordinated with this shift in corporate culture, with the responsibility for bringing innovative and creative solutions to our clients belonging to everyone in the firm, Kahler Slater not only survived the loss of David's talent, but also has grown and prospered since, including being named to the national Best Places to Work list for small and medium businesses for each of the six years since the Great Place to Work® Institute created the program. David's understanding of the design of buildings as a collaborative venture extended to the redesign and transformation of the organization that still bears his name.

In keeping with this philosophy for design excellence, we identify our design superstars as team members who help others succeed. *Coaching and mentoring others* is another key criterion to qualify to join the ranks of owners at the firm.

Our Teams Feel Safe

Creativity can be a nerve-wracking journey, even on a good day. We know that innovation occurs when people are allowed and even encouraged to take risks, and doing so can be scary. Whether you're designing a new building or transforming your enterprise to be more consistent with your authentic vision, you are daring to dream of something that has yet to exist. There is much at stake: peoples' futures, perhaps millions of dollars, internal political struggles, the possibility that feelings might get hurt, the potential for rejection, and so forth. There is also the frustration that comes with ambiguity, false starts, multiple iterations. Our people need to be able to trust that we'll stand by them, even if it means having to go toe-to-toe with a client.

If our staff knows that we are devoted to helping them do their best work, to really give life to their passions, they can then focus on sharing with their clients their talents and expertise—the best they can possibly offer. Fortunately, we do our best work when we work with clients who share our same Core Beliefs and Values. When their world view is the same as ours, these tend to become our best projects, because trust and confidence in the entire team (which ultimately includes the clients themselves) help everyone to invest their energies on the project, not on self-protection.

Our Work Areas Are Designed to Promote Collaboration

In our own corporate offices, we have designed our environments to be as open and transparent as possible. Our Team Collaboration Spaces (our conference rooms where meetings take place) feature whiteboards and pinup space, and are fronted in glass to encourage people walking by to check out what's going on inside. You won't see enclosed offices, but you will see centralized café and kitchen spaces to encourage people to get up from their desks to get coffee, or share a birthday treat, and in the process, engage with their fellow creatives. Centralized copy workrooms provide opportunities for similar casual interactions throughout the day. And at our headquarters office, you'll find the *Kahler Slater Experience*—our pontoon boat docked right outside our back door. We call it our floating conference room, and it's available to all staff for their use during the summer months.

CONCLUSION

Granted, depending on your enterprise, you may not think of your staff as creatives, in the pure sense of the word, as we do at Kahler Slater. But every team has a creative component to it, especially in modern times when product design and customer service depend on innovation, on-the-spot original thinking, and devotion to quality. And as you are undergoing a transformation to create—or recreate—an authentic enterprise built on a shared vision, your people have definitely joined the ranks of creatives. They're helping you design something that has never before existed.

As such, they deserve leadership that is up to the challenge of creating a safe culture in which everyone can collaborate openly, safely, and creatively. It can be done!

Chapter 5

DISCOVER—WHERE ARE YOU TODAY?

Discovery consists of seeing what everybody has seen and thinking what nobody has thought.

Albert Szent-Gyorgyi

Photo by Pixland/Media Bakery.

Discover

Throughout the first part of this book, we have been focusing on the multiple advantages of creating an organization that integrates the four key elements of total experience design. You've seen what your enterprise might be capable of if you were able to truly bring all the key components together into one unified vision. So now the next question has got to be: How do you actually do that?

You are about to start a journey through the 5Ds (Discover, Dream, Define, Design, Deliver). Your destination: A more authentic enterprise with a clear vision of what you want to represent to all your stakeholders and exactly how that authenticity will show up in your stakeholders' lives in terms of experiences. At this stage of the process, you may not yet know precisely what that vision is and all the details that will manifest that vision. (If you don't, you will after you complete the Dream phase described in Chapter 6.) But still, you need to know who you are now to all your stakeholders, how they are experiencing your organization, and even how your organization compares with similar players in your field.

Welcome to the Discover phase, the first of the 5Ds. With Discover, your journey toward your ideal future begins.

The journey metaphor is an apt one. This step is very much like planning a trip, in which you must understand where you are before being able to determine where you're going. Say you'd like to travel to Paris. How could you plan your trip to France if you don't even know where you're starting from? How would you know which mode of transportation to use if you're not certain of your current location and situation? Will you fly? Can you drive? Take the train? Likewise, the Discover phase generates a complete analysis of your current lay of the land before you venture forward into new territory, and before you choose the strategies you need to actually get to the correct destination. Who are you? Where have you been? What vision have you developed that drives your business forward?

As you start on your own organizational transformation, you must first know how your organization serves your customers and community today. And, of course, you want to achieve this understanding according to the 4P matrix to make sure that the entire picture of your business is an integrated one. What *Perception* does your business have in the marketplace? How well do your *People* represent who you are and what you are about? What *Products and Services* do you produce right now as a result of your processes? And, of course, how does your *Place* support and make manifest your authentic vision for your organization?

There are several Discover tools that will help you fully understand and document the current condition in which your organization exists. They can be grouped into three main categories: Observation (i.e., where you, as the researcher, or a third party are observing your organization or the organization of others from a distance); Engagement (where researchers are directly interacting with your people); and Collaboration (where the researchers seek out external examples, organizations, or people for insights).

OBSERVATION

Fresh Eyes Audit

During the Fresh Eyes Audit, you bring in an outsider to serve as a fly on the wall of your organization. (Don't try to do this yourself. You already know the people and processes of your organization too well. And, if you are a leader in your organization, the behavior of your staff naturally is likely to change—most likely to improve—when they're around you. You need a stranger—someone who can unobtrusively observe the goings on in your business or organization.)

Give your staff advance warning that there will be a person or two hanging around, shooting pictures or video and taking notes. Let them know this person has your permission to do so, and that they should just ignore him or her. Eventually the observer will disappear into the background of the busy day, and he or she can take thorough notes while your staffers lose themselves in their familiar daily activities. Your researchers should be completely in the background, just watching and noting the details of the way your organization operates. They should never interject themselves into your employees' day—not even as *pretend* customers. This is how their observations might cover all 4Ps.

Perception. An onsite observer might overhear customers talking about your establishment. That would be an indication of the community's perception of your business. But you also might gain an additional understanding of your word of mouth by conducting a review of public reports of your business or neighborhood via newspapers or online publications, or reviews of your product or service. Additionally, on-site observers will be looking for evidence that your messaging—advertising, communications, marketing, and so forth, both internally and externally—is consistent with your vision, culture, and brand. If your marketing campaign claims that you have the friendliest service providers around, but it is observed that people working at your headquarters seem engaged in hand-to-hand combat, there's a disconnect that needs to be addressed if you and your staff want to live an authentic organizational life.

People.   How well do your employees represent the brand that you want to present to your stakeholders? Are your employees friendly and relaxed, but professional? Does their level of formality match the formality (or informality) that you want your customers to experience when they engage with your organization? Do they treat each other respectfully? Are they welcoming to your clients, customers, and other stakeholders? Do your managers treat their direct reports with respect? Is your business sufficiently staffed to handle your customers quickly and courteously? Are your staff living, breathing, and authentic examples of your Vision Statement and your Core Beliefs and Values in action?

Products and Services.   What does the observer see when your people are making your products and/or delivering services? If your organization is a hospital, for instance, how quickly and compassionately are patients admitted? If you run a hotel, will the observer see carefully made beds and clean bathrooms? What condition are your towels in? Is the furniture in good repair? If you run a restaurant, is your food consistent with your promise? If you advertise, for example, fresh and authentic Italian cuisine, is it really? Or is there a faint metallic aftertaste from the can?

Place.   Is your place of business clean? Well-lit? Organized? Safe? Are the restrooms clean? Is it easy to find parking? Does your property look well cared for? What does it sound like, smell like, or feel like in your facility? Does its appearance convey the message that you care about everyone who does business with your organization? Does it send the right messages to all who visit or work there? Are your authentic culture and values made physically manifest in a way that helps people to understand who you are and what you're about?

A Fresh Eyes Audit can reveal many disconnects that are easily overlooked by people who work within the environment every day. For instance, when a major national retail organization announced a new tagline for its retail operations, it wanted to ensure that the value proposition offered by the tagline to customers was something that its own employees experienced and embraced as well. To determine if the external messaging was in sync with staff perceptions and experiences, the company commissioned a Fresh Eyes Audit at its headquarters.

During the audit, an external researcher documented her observations of the workplace by photographing existing conditions, including key areas of interaction such as employee workstations, cafeteria, lobby, and break areas. She also documented how visitors and vendors were treated by reception staff to see if the initial guest experience was consistent with and reinforced by the brand message articulated by the organization.

The audit revealed that the workplace did not consistently express the value proposition of the tagline. The researcher later described the general feel of the workplace as DilbertLand, with row upon row of drab cubicles with tall, solid partitions in a vast, nondescript space. There was no sense of individuality or creative inspiration. The only way a visitor could tell which department was which was by the heaps of merchandise samples spilling out of boxes. The place was uninspiring (which was in direct contrast to what the new tagline was intended to express), and rather monotonous, giving perhaps the impression of being disorganized and disheveled, even if it wasn't. While some might be surprised that a large and successful organization with vibrant, well-designed retail environments would not place equal importance on the vitality of its own headquarters, this is not an uncommon experience for many workplaces. Not because organizations intend their employees to work in boring, poorly maintained, or less-than-ideal environments, but because often they simply don't see it. Or they are under pressure to hold down or cut costs. And they fail to realize that investing in employee comfort or pleasant work conditions brings a return on investment which includes increased employee satisfaction, creativity, and pride—all of which have a dramatic impact on the bottom line.

The Fresh Eyes Audit provides information beyond what we can see. Experiences are multisensory, which anyone who has visited a hospital or restaurant can certainly appreciate. The sense of smell obviously plays a role in the way we experience most anything in our lives. But the sense of hearing is also important. During a hospital sound study, similar to a Fresh Eyes Audit (which might more appropriately be called Fresh Ears Audit), a Kahler Slater researcher noticed that one of the nurses carried a large collection of keys—which made an immense amount of noise when she walked down the patient corridor. But the nurse had stopped hearing the sound. As a result of this discovery, however, the design team incorporated a quiet card key system in the new hospital design. In the same hospital, another sound study researcher suffered through a constant beeping for more than 45 minutes late one night. When she asked a nurse what that sound was, she learned it was an alarm that indicated an empty IV bag needed replacing. But it still took a nurse an additional 20 minutes to change the bag. This audit revealed a very serious operations issue. It was just a matter of bringing in *fresh ears* to have a good listen.

Seeing (or hearing, smelling, touching, even tasting) things that others can't or don't is why a Fresh Eyes Audit is such a valuable first step in the 5D Process. You probably know this phenomenon firsthand. If you've ever sold a home, you may have had the experience of meeting with a real estate professional who assesses your property to set a price before it goes on the market. The broker probably pointed out things to you that you'd simply stopped noticing, especially if you'd been in the house for a few years. Sure, you've been meaning to paint the dining room walls, or fix that leaky faucet, or trim back the overgrown bush in the front yard. But in your day-to-day life, these little chores have taken a back seat to more pressing projects and expectations. So they have gone undone. And they mount up almost imperceptibly as your attention is usually focused elsewhere. Do these things really matter when it comes to attracting a buyer? Any good real estate professional will tell you that the answer is "yes." A loose tile here. Evidence of water damage there. Hideously outdated wallpaper everywhere. It takes away from the ability of your house to say, "Buy me."

Similarly, overlooked flaws in the way your business presents itself take away from the power of your organization to broadcast the message: "Do business with me." So fresh eyes are in order to help you spot those details to which you might have become oblivious over time. Not only is it bad for business to remain ignorant about these details (who wants to have their merchandise represented by a retailer that can't even keep its own corporate headquarters well organized?) but the lost opportunity cost of failing to use your facility to create the kinds of experiences that motivate employees and send the right messages to prospective employees, vendors, clients, and other guests is also very high.

Literature Research

Just as you might have been so busy that you have failed to notice the slow decline of your physical workplace and the experiences within, you might have failed to notice gradual but significant changes in your field, market, or among your stakeholders. Are they older? Younger? Have advances in technology made them more independent? Or do they need your expertise even more, but just in a different way? Has your kind of enterprise gone global with different business models showing more effective success strategies than the ones you've been using in recent years? What about legislation or other public policy changes that might influence the decisions you make around your organization? Much of this essential information can be captured in a literature research (books, publications, and Web sites from your main professional associations, as well as academic papers). Initial literature research can be done without engaging your stakeholders.

ENGAGEMENT

The Experience Audit

The Experience Audit is the process in which the observers do inject themselves into the doings of the organization. A common Experience

Audit with which most people are familiar is the *secret shopper*, in which individuals are paid to pose as average, everyday buyers and systematically evaluate their shopping experiences. However, the Experience Audit can be taken to some very interesting extremes to obtain valuable insights.

For instance, when a community hospital was considering an addition to its surgical wing, an Experience Audit of the existing wing was conducted to see what the current patient experience was like and what improvements could be made through renovation and new construction. Two outsiders posed as husband (Jeff) and wife (Sharon), with Sharon about to be admitted for arthroscopic knee surgery. Most of the frontline staff responsible for direct caregiving, including the anesthesiologist who called Sharon the night before the scheduled surgery, were unaware that this experience was a simulation. (Importantly for these two auditors, however, the physician who was slated to conduct the surgery was in on the audit.)

The audit, which began the evening before the surgery and concluded in the operating room just moments before the surgery was to commence, uncovered a number of interesting 4P observations—both good and bad. Jeff and Sharon noted that the extensive, well-maintained, and beautiful landscaping surrounding the building served as a calming influence during the drive to the front entry. (Sharon may have simulated the need for the surgery, but the butterflies in her stomach were very real.) Indeed, Sharon noted later in her report that this same view of the landscape was the last thing that she saw through a large window as she was wheeled into the surgical suite, which she found to be a pleasant distraction that calmed her nerves. Unfortunately, the cramped and cluttered operating suite and recovery room had just the opposite effect.

Another uncomfortable moment happened just as the couple entered the hospital lobby. The smell of freshly made popcorn coming from a popcorn cart adjacent to the lobby filled the air. Fresh popcorn, of course, is better than that typical *anesthetic meets cleaning products* hospital smell. But, for Sharon, who had been told not to eat anything after midnight of the previous evening (a common instruction to patients about to undergo surgery), the popcorn smell intensified her hunger and added to her feelings of being uncomfortable.

As the audit progressed, yet another moment contributed to Sharon's uneasiness and fear. After she was prepped and ready for surgery, she and Jeff were riding in the elevator together with a couple of staff members. When the elevator came to a stop, both the front and rear doors of the elevator opened. Jeff was instructed to exit one way into the waiting room, while Sharon was wheeled the opposite way into the surgical area. As Sharon noted later in her report to the hospital: "It was impossible, under the circumstances, for us to have a 'goodbye moment.' Indeed, if he had felt comfortable whispering a few words of encouragement into my ear, or even giving me a kiss goodbye in the cramped elevator with two strangers watching, there simply was no preparation to do so, and no time to react. The doors opened, and Jeff was pointed in one direction, while I was whisked away in another. This only increased my feeling of being nervous, and being alone, which might have been mitigated through the verbal or physical reassurance of my husband."

Other disconnects between the hospital's intention of patient and family service and the actual experience included the pager that Jeff was given to let him know when Sharon's surgery was complete. In theory, the idea of having a pager, which allows family and friends to leave the waiting area and get a cup of coffee in the cafeteria or use a restroom, seems like a good idea. But in practice, the range of the pager covered only a very short radius from the waiting room. Since it was a beautiful day, Jeff decided to step outside for some fresh air and to take in more of the beautiful surroundings. He was surprised to find that the range of the pager stopped at the doors of the hospital. This prevented him from going outside, else he risk missing being notified of Sharon's progress.

While many of these observations and disconnects may seem minor, they can add up to a less-than-positive experience. Fortunately, many, if not most, of these disconnects are relatively simple and often inexpensive to fix. All that is required for the experience to be dramatically improved is a heightened and empathetic awareness of the experience from the patient's or client's point of view, and a simple change in behavior or operational procedure on the part of the caregiver or service provider. Experience Audits can help you get the fresh perspective necessary to see those disconnects that might not have occurred to you otherwise.

Competition Audit

The Competition Audit measures how well your competitors are delivering the experiences they are promising to their intended audiences. This kind of information helps you capitalize on your organization's perceived or actual strengths—and eliminate or minimize its weaknesses.

For instance, as Paul Berlin was beginning to brainstorm ideas about opening Sabor in Milwaukee, there were already approximately 110 *churrascarias* in the United States—each with its own interpretation and expression of the *churrascaria* experience. He took his experience design team to several locations in Chicago to acquaint the group with the various design and operational approaches of these would-be competitors. Visiting these venues and experiencing firsthand what they offered helped differentiate the Sabor environment and experience *eatertainment* for Milwaukee and Wisconsin.

By engaging as a customer of his competition, Berlin quickly identified the ways in which he wanted his *churrascaria* to be different. Some of the competing restaurants, he felt, were architecturally overdesigned to the point of being visually cluttered, so there was really no feeling of an overarching design concept that flowed through the space. Based on what Berlin and his team observed at his competitors' establishments, he intentionally went the other way, deciding instead to create a relaxed, yet elegant atmosphere in which everything is subtle and pleasing. This way, the customers can focus on what they really came for—a memorable meal. It was this choice that created the differentiating factor for Sabor and authentically separated this *churrascaria* from its competition. Berlin would not have had that epiphany without having had the firsthand experience of the Competition Audit.

Any current experience or process that is critical to your organization's successful delivery of its vision—whether that be a staff orientation process, a front desk or admissions experience, or a prospective student college tour, to name but a few, can be audited. The results can help you quickly gauge where you are currently, and where you need to be headed as an organization.

COLLABORATION

Benchmarking

With Competition and Experience Audits, you and your team must behave somewhat like spies, gathering information without the subject knowing what you're up to. In contrast, benchmarking puts you in the position of openly collaborating with your counterparts—even your competition—with the idea that shared knowledge improves everyone's understanding and prospects for success. Part of knowing where you are in your current business circumstances is knowing where other people like you are in *their* businesses. How are they achieving their objectives and goals? In a benchmarking project, you can be open about your curiosity about the operations of other organizations. In fact, your counterparts in other organizations may welcome your request to share information and insights because it offers *them* the opportunity to see what you're doing right and well. Done properly, benchmarking can be the rising tide that lifts all boats. Unless you're in a zero-sum game industry, in which there can be only one winner, benchmarking can help boost everyone's success prospects, without anyone feeling as though they are losing their competitive edge. Why? Because you will be so differentiated by your authenticity that you won't really consider other players in your space to be true competitors.

You can also use benchmarking to investigate the practices of similar companies or industries that are unrelated to yours. For instance, when the Marquette University School of Dentistry decided that it wanted to learn about practices that could help it become more patient-friendly and student-centered, the faculty and administration didn't have other dentistry schools to learn from, as they were creating an entirely new vision for a new curriculum and environment to better teach students how to become dentists. So they visited Shawano Hospital in Shawano, Wisconsin. This hospital is part of a growing network of health care facilities dedicated to patient-centered care. Run by the Planetree Alliance in Connecticut (and named after the sycamore, or planetree, which is the tree Hippocrates was said to have sat under while teaching), this membership affiliation answers to rigorous standards of patient-centered care and practices. It's one thing for a hospital to have these standards. It's an entirely different matter altogether to replicate them in the context of a dental school. But the first step in that direction was to visit a Planetree hospital and find out exactly what they did, and then to borrow from these examples.

So, a group of Marquette faculty, staff, administrators, and experience design team members boarded a bus and headed north for a few hours to spend the day touring the hospital and meeting with hospital staff to discover how they designed and delivered healing experiences and environments for patients and their families that were centered on their special wants and needs.

The result for the Marquette University School of Dentistry? Shawano Hospital, designed completely around the notion of attending to the needs of its patients and their families as a primary focus, served as one of the sources of inspiration for the Marquette faculty as they designed not only a new building, but also an entirely new curriculum. This new teaching modality emphasized a patient-centered approach, in which the students followed the same patients throughout their treatment, rather than handing off a patient to a different student every time they came in.

"The way patient care was managed before, the patient assignments were arranged according to the clinical discipline: fillings, periodontal treatment, etc. As a result, the patient was treated like a commodity who may not have ever seen the same student dentist more than once," said Dean William Lobb, the visionary leader who oversaw the design overhaul.

"When we decided to build the building and recreate the programming, we were going to zero-based curriculum," said Lobb. "Whatever we had in the past we weren't necessarily going to have anymore. We were starting with a blank piece of paper. If we had tinkered around the edges, we would never have gotten the changes we did get."

What they got was a learning environment that is supportive and positive, as opposed to the previous school, where the students were put under stress, taking multiple independent courses—some of which were redundant and all of which were taught in silos with little attention paid as to how the various aspects of these courses related to each other. The previous environment also held the students back in terms of learning more up-to-date skills and technologies.

"We were always complaining that we didn't have enough time to teach the newer techniques that had come into common use in dentistry," Lobb said. "But there was plenty of time hidden in our curriculum. We were limited by our monolithic curriculum and stagnated ways of doing things."

It was this change, this new way of teaching and learning, that subsequently drove the design of a new facility. The new curriculum and school currently serve as an international benchmark for dental schools, as faculty from other dental programs now come to Marquette to tour their facility for inspiration.

The Marquette University School of Dentistry offers an innovative teaching and learning experience and environment. *Photo by Steve Hall, Hedrich Blessing.*

Your counterpart companies that are suitable for benchmarking studies can be found in a variety of groups, without putting anyone in the position of having to give away trade secrets. You can benchmark companies in the same industries, even the same communities. If you're a nonprofit, you can talk with other nonprofits about how they solve their mission-critical objectives. Or better yet, talk with for-profits and borrow lessons from them. You can even benchmark with head-to-head competitors. In Silicon Valley, for instance, high-tech companies are locked in a pitched battle over resources: funding, talent, market share, even real estate. But the human resources community is an extremely tight one, as high potential HR professionals circulate through many of the same companies throughout the Bay Area. As a result, long-timers know each other, have worked with each other, and have worked for each other as the years progressed. And so, they are surprisingly open with their talent strategies. The result: the Bay Area is a magnet for some of the world's most innovative individuals, who collectively design the future through technology. Much of that strength is built through benchmarking.

Reach out to as broad a variety of excellent companies or organizations as you can and have time for. Find out how they're solving problems, and be willing to share with them how you are solving problems that they might have. This kind of knowledge sharing won't threaten your competitive edge, it will only sharpen it.

Surveys and Focus Groups

You know something needs to change, and you have a pretty good idea what that is. In fact, you're absolutely certain. And you might be entirely wrong. You need the input of your stakeholders to help you make sure that you're targeting the correct flaws and disconnects as you go after improving and better integrating your 4P offerings. This is where surveys and focus groups come in. By capturing the opinions and attitudes of your current clients and employees, you'll uncover the necessary insights and wishes that you might have overlooked entirely. In articulating your current condition, it's helpful to discover how those who regularly interact with your organization think and feel about their current experiences. Surveying the opinions, thoughts, and attitudes of current clients and employees and/or asking for their direct feedback helps you gain valuable insights into the here and now of an organization.

For instance, a community college wanted to improve the overall student experience on campus. So the administrators surveyed students, faculty, and staff to better understand their current satisfaction or dissatisfaction with life on campus and decide what to improve and what strengths to leverage. Some 1,100 students, faculty, staff, and administrators responded to the Web-based survey during the three weeks it was online. One of the areas of the survey focus was the existing student union, where many of the students went to hang out between classes, since there are no dorms on this campus. As was the case with this college, student unions typically serve as the hub of a campus, and as such they are generally very active and energetic places. The survey revealed that students at this particular college (many of whom are older than the more traditional college student), tended to be commuters who also typically work full- and part-time jobs while attending classes, and as such, were interested in a less stimulating experience. What they wanted in their student union, rather than a bustling hub, was an oasis of calm, a place they could go to unwind, relax, take a nap, or spend a quiet moment.

In another instance, a public university about to begin the design of a new recreational facility on campus for students and faculty held focus groups to discover what students wanted in the new building. The assumption was that students would be interested in additional fitness programs and amenities—more action, more sports—but the focus groups said that what they really wanted was a place to unwind from the stresses of college life. Treadmills were fine, but what these students really wanted were pool tables and massage therapy!

Surveys and focus groups don't always have to be scientifically rigorous, with questions that can be statistically validated. They can be casual, even fun, and still garner valuable information. The design of the Monster.com headquarters in Maynard, Massachusetts, was intended to tell the story of a young, growing, high technology business in part by using the monster theme that represents the organization. And who knows more about monsters than children? So the design team surveyed the children in their lives about the habits and habitats of monsters. As to the question of where monsters live, the most common answer was "under beds and in closets." As a result, a monster is painted inside the closet off the reception area at the corporate headquarters of one of the nation's leading job search services.

In a similar vein, Badger Meter, an international manufacturer and marketer of industrial and water meters, was trying to get a quick snapshot of its culture. The question was asked of senior leadership: "If Badger Meter was a beer, what kind of beer would it be and why?" Within a few minutes, the group agreed that the 104-year-old company culture was like a Guinness: hearty, solid, flavorful, and robust. It has been around for a long time, so it's proven, reliable, and consistent, and will never do you wrong. You'll know what you're getting—there are no surprises. At the same time, it's not flashy or frothy. And it speaks of quality. In less than five minutes, a snapshot of the organization came into view that might not have surfaced as quickly or in such rich detail as might occur in a more traditional focus group setting or survey. Any kind of metaphor can be used in this way. Types of shoes, cars, or candy are interesting and thought-provoking ones to try.

The Discover phase lays the foundation for the rest of the Ds. It's an essential phase of the process—not to be skipped. It might be tempting, though, because the next D—Dream—is where the real innovation begins.

Chapter 6

DREAM—WHERE DO YOU WANT TO GO TOMORROW?

Hold a picture of yourself long and steadily enough in your mind's eye and you will be drawn toward it. Picture yourself vividly as winning and that alone will contribute immeasurably to success. Great living starts with a picture, held in your imagination, of what you would like to do or be.

Harry Emerson Fosdick

Photo by Photodisc/Media Bakery.

DREAM

The second D—Dream—is your chance to blow out the walls of your perhaps limiting assumptions of what's possible and bring your project or organization into the world of the ideal future. This is where you leave your constraints, budgets, and limitations at the door—for the time being, anyway. This is the time to allow yourself to go beyond anything and everything you imagined before, to begin your journey into the rarified air of *wow!*

This is where—with the help of your team of key stakeholders—you discover the vision for your future. And attach to it a menu of multisensory experiences to make that vision come alive. Unmistakably. Consistently. Specifically. Inspiringly. Authentically.

The Dream phase centers on the Visioning Workshop, which is the heart of the Dream process and experience. By the time the workshop is over, all the participants will hold in their minds the same, integrated experience vision, which is a story or set of stories that describes the ideal total experience in multidimensional, multisensory terms.

WHO PARTICIPATES

This participatory, consensus-building workshop is attended by the top leaders of the organization who collectively represent each of the 4Ps. In addition to the C-suite (CEO, CFO, COO), this typically includes the heads of marketing and sales (Perception), human resources (People), customer relations and product development (Products and Services), and facilities management (Place).

Other key stakeholders in the organization—staff, customers, board members, community representatives, and sometimes even project financial donors—may be invited to attend the Visioning Workshop. Depending on the size of the organization and the task at hand, workshops can be as small as 4 or 5 people, or involve as many as 150 in a single session. If the organizational culture demands it, there can be separate Visioning Workshops for senior leaders and the rest of the staff. However, in most cases, it's best that staff representatives at all levels are included, and that they participate in the same Visioning Workshop as their leadership. This way, everyone emerges with the same vision in their minds, created by the unifying experience of participating in the session together. What is essential is that everyone who will be responsible for manifesting the resulting vision will have the opportunity to contribute to what that vision will ultimately be. This group could also include patients, customers, community planners—anyone who will be a partner in or recipient of how your organization delivers successful total experiences. If these stakeholders play an essential role in manifesting your ideal vision—even if they are on the receiving end of your organization's offerings—you may find their voice and contribution to the Visioning Workshop to be invaluable. You will hear what they want in their own words and see what they want through their own eyes. In addition, you won't have to go through the exhausting task of having to achieve their buy-in when the time comes to roll out your new vision. You will already have the most powerful idea evangelists onboard—your stakeholders themselves. And there are no better people to tell you when you're being fake, or that the experiences you're designing won't work. Because no matter how brilliant you think a new total experience offering may be, it simply won't work if the people who will deliver it are incapable or unwilling to do so.

The multidisciplinary nature of each working group is also key to its success. As representatives of each of the 4Ps work together to design ideal total experiences, they each bring a valuable perspective of and expertise in their respective areas of responsibility. Bringing that experience to the table and working together, the group will avoid the all-too-familiar scenario of the right hand not knowing what the left is doing. Instead, by sharing what they each know, they'll have a much better chance of collectively developing integrated and more holistic total experiences. For example, the way in which a prospective customer becomes aware of and interested in an organization due to an advertising campaign sets the stage for the delivery of the product or service by the people who represent the company. Each of these areas depends on the other. And if one falls short, all suffer.

This same principle goes for making sure the CEO (and other senior-most leaders) is also part of the Visioning Workshop. If you anticipate having to make a formal presentation to any individual after the session is over (to get his or her approval and sign-off on the next steps, for example), bring this person into the session from the very beginning. Make your key staff part of the visioning experience so they can own the outcomes.

Visionary leaders typically love the Dream phase because it helps them articulate ideas they may have been struggling with for years. In the Dream phase, they can pull together all their hopes and dreams for their enterprise in a way that they can actually take action on them, with highly differentiating and authentic results that are integrated by aligned 4Ps. This process encourages and supports them by painting a clear picture of the future—which is essential to making it a reality.

And from the point of view of the rest of the stakeholders (staffers, community representatives, customers), it's a chance for them to finally see their leader's vision and to contribute their own ideas and insights to enhance that original idea. As a team, they are thus prepared to make that dream come true. Those who create it, own it. And those who own it are most likely to do whatever it takes to make sure that vision comes true.

Ideally, in the Dream phase, the team requires an outside facilitator to prompt brainstorming by asking the right questions of the right people at the right time. In the Dream phase, some of the most important answers emerge when the question "What if . . . ?" is asked by a master facilitator whose objectivity allows him or her to create a safe place for stakeholders to take a step back and see possibilities through new eyes. A good facilitator knows how to engage even the most reluctant participants in the group, and how to keep the interaction going. Good facilitators are flexible. They must be able to roll with the punches (or the unexpected), and they aren't afraid to ask the dumb question or offer the weird idea, knowing that this interaction often prompts new discussion that leads to better, more creative ideas.

SETTING THE STAGE

The Visioning Workshops must be collaborative from the very start, with a creative atmosphere designed to evoke the desired total experiences that you will want to share ultimately with your clients and customers. If, for instance, you want to create a high-end spa, hold your workshop in a beautifully appointed room with candles and soft fragrances. Why not invite participants to get comfortable by putting on a pair of spa slippers? What better way to create the future than to immerse yourself in it from the very beginning as much as possible?

From the invitations sent to the prospective participants, to the music played during the session, to the food and the room décor, to the exercises used during the session—these are all touchpoints of the total experience you will strive to achieve as a result of the workshop itself. Immersing participants in the future in a multisensory way helps them to experience it in a more tangible way. And for those who are resistant to change or are skeptical, it makes the future less of a scary place. It also begins to spark the imagination of those involved.

With careful planning and a little creativity, you can use any space to evoke the feeling of the end result or experience you're seeking to create. You can even turn a conference room into a luxurious apartment. For instance, we once met with a client team working to bring a contemporary housing experience—a new, high-end, high-rise condominium project—to Milwaukee. This was at the beginning of the downtown condominium boom in Milwaukee, which was part of a renaissance along the waterfront of Lake Michigan. Wealthy Baby Boomers were cashing in on their five-bedroom colonial family homes in the suburbs after their kids headed off to college. And they were eager to buy snazzy new condos in the city's revitalized downtown area.

The project team included the developer and the developer's associates, the general contractor, and the local business people who were the primary investors in the venture (one of whom served as the primary salesperson for the development). Each of the primary investors personally intended to purchase a unit in the new development. The question before us all was what would this development actually be like? What would the *experience* of living in this new development be for the residents there? As might be expected, each of the team members had a different idea of what the project could be, including the investor most responsible for the sales effort. However, everyone seemed to agree that they wanted the experience to be upscale, classy, and high-end, and to maximize the lakefront location of the site.

But *upscale, classy,* and *high-end* could mean different things to different people. To get everyone imagining the same experience in a world that didn't exist yet, we held a Visioning Workshop at Kahler Slater's Milwaukee headquarters. After we had gathered the group in one of our more typical conference rooms for what they expected would be a brief kickoff meeting, we told them that we needed to move to a different locale, one more *worthy* of a discussion of this special project. We led the group to a specially transformed conference room, designed specifically to transport the team in its collective imagination to a venue that could serve as a benchmark for the project to come.

When the team entered that room, they left behind the business world of the office building we were in and entered an elegant dinner party in someone's very private and exclusive home. Inside the room, the conference table was dressed in fine white linen table cloths and gleaming silver candelabra, replicating the experience of entering a well-heeled friend's chic, modern dining room, perhaps on New York's tony Upper East Side. On the table, elegant selections of hors d'oeuvres and champagne were artfully arranged. The room was lit only by the candles and soft jazz music was playing in the background to further set the mood.

After some time enjoying the refreshments and mingling, almost as though the team truly was at a dinner party, the project manager took center stage, welcoming the group to his "New York condo" and telling the group that he had just signed a contract to purchase a similar condo in Milwaukee. Turning to the investor who had been selling the project based upon a vision that was his alone, he asked the investor to share with the group, in the same way he had shared with the project manager, his sales pitch for the new Milwaukee condo. "You are all my New York friends, and I'd like you to be my Milwaukee neighbors," said the project manager. "So I'd like you to hear the sales pitch that sold me." At which point, the investor/salesperson began to speak passionately and eloquently to the group, sharing his sales pitch, which allowed the rest of the group to truly understand for the first time what the vision for the project was (at least according to the investor/pitchman).

After a discussion to get all of the team members on the same page, the project manager announced that it was now years into the future, the group was back in Milwaukee, and the new condo tower was complete. We brought up the lights to reveal a gigantic panorama of downtown Milwaukee overlooking Lake Michigan on one of the large walls of the transformed conference room. This is the view that future condominium owners would expect to see when looking out the windows of their new homes. And so this transformed conference room "beamed" the development team to a future time and place where their collective vision already would have been made manifest. From that transformative setting, they were able to put their imaginations to work to fill in the details of their vision made manifest—which included increasing the project budget by 20 percent to account for a shared vision that was more luxurious than each investor alone had imagined. Understanding these heightened expectations and resulting cost increases at the beginning of the project made it easier for the clients to make design decisions and choices during the course of the project.

This kind of transformative setting also can be conducive to a little bit of role-playing to get the Dream team in the right frame of mind. With another client in need of public support and government financing for a potentially controversial development, we set up a "press conference" scenario. Kahler Slater staffers took on the roles of key community opinion leaders during our first meeting with the clients. The design team turned into a "newspaper reporter," a "mayor," and "county board supervisors," with someone playing the role of an "interested citizen," as they questioned the clients about the new development at a mock news conference we set up in our office, "announcing" the new venture. The experience design team heard about the vision these clients had in their heads for the new development, as well as how they planned to deal with the obstacles facing the deal—the media, government officials hesitant about using public financing for the project, and so forth. This also led to a discussion about how we could help the developers in building consensus and excitement about the project, since even the best projects mean nothing if there is no support to deliver them.

The transformative setting doesn't have to be this elaborate, of course. Anything you can do to remove the day-to-day contexts and associations that your participants bring will help open their minds to new possibilities. At the very least, try to hold the workshop in a room away from their own place of business—with explicit instructions that cell phones and PDAs are not allowed during the workshop. If you can identify a retreat destination that comes close to evoking the overall feeling of the desired outcome, so much the better. For one large midwestern grocery store chain client, for example, who wanted to create a more European approach to grocery shopping, akin to what one might find at an open-air market in a small country village, we chose a Tuscan-style villa as the setting for the workshop. The villa was surrounded by an outdoor courtyard and beautiful gardens, similar to what one might find at a country market in a small, quaint, centuries-old Italian village. The change of scenery helped the participants transport themselves out of their daily corporate environment to an entirely new setting that inspired new ideas throughout the day. And even experience for themselves—if only slightly—the kinds of experiences they wanted to share with their customers.

One final note regarding setting the stage: Be sure you have set up a designated *parking lot board*. This is a blackboard, whiteboard, or large easel pad that holds or *parks* the random ideas and questions that are bound to pop up throughout the session. These often are comments, questions, or ideas that don't have any place in the conversation of the moment, but they are still important enough to be recorded for review at the end of the day—if they're not already addressed during the course of the session. Not only are these valuable tidbits that need to be captured, but also it's important that the participants know they're being heard and their contributions are respected—even if they are somewhat out of place at the moment. It allows them, as well as their fellow participants, to relax and focus on the task at hand. And it allows the facilitator to continue moving the process and discussion forward.

THE TOOLS

Visioning Workshops are designed to inspire innovative ideas, and having fun goes a long way toward doing just that. As such, participants should have plenty of toys available to help them unleash their creativity: Legos™, soap bubbles, Etch-a-Sketches™, party hats, feather boas, crayons, drawing paper,

Play-Doh™. The more buttoned-up executives may struggle with loosening up and playing with props—especially in front of their subordinates. But even the most reluctant of leaders who have taken part in Kahler Slater Dream exercises report later that they see the value of what appears to be child's play. (See Chapter 8 for additional commentary on the power of play.) Fun is an essential part of releasing work-hardened minds into the fields of innovation and possibility. And so this is the time to give the participants tools to encourage their creative sides and let their imaginations soar.

ORGANIZING THE GROUPS

Much of the work developed in the workshops is done through small group activity. Ideally, these groups should be no larger than five to seven participants each, with each group having an odd number of people (in the event you need a tie breaker on a vote or exercise). According to the book *Team-based Learning*, studies dating back to the 1950s on the topic of the appropriate size of problem-solving groups indicate that larger groups generally have more resources and are thus better equipped to solve complex problems. But the larger the group, the less likely that all members will actually participate and take ownership in the outcome.[1] As stated by the authors, "In terms of actual numbers, most researchers have concluded that for significant intellectual work, the minimum size for an effective group is five members . . . most studies have concluded that groups larger than seven members tend to encounter significant problems with group processes."

It is important to mix each group in terms of gender, ethnicity, position within the organization, experience, personality type (e.g., introverts and extroverts), and so forth. The idea is to make each group as interdisciplinary and diverse as possible, so that participants will feed off of each other's unique perspective on the organization and the breakthrough ideas that will emerge in the session. The more diverse each group is, the better the chances of generating truly creative and innovative ideas.

The correlation between diversity and creativity has been tracked in very interesting ways. For instance, in one study by the American Institute of Architects, 50 architects were asked to work under a prescribed set of conditions to test different ideas for working collaboratively. A planning team organized the 50 architects into 10 five-person teams, which were purposely diverse, based upon the experience, skills, and personality types of the various participants. Each team also included a student observer from the University of Cincinnati or Ball State University, whose role included observing group interaction, convening discussion about the process (but not the result), reporting on what he or she observed, and encouraging participants to share their own observations on the experience.

The assignment for each group was to develop design ideas for Cincinnati's Downtown Gateway program, which celebrates civic history, provides orientation for visitors, and seeks to highlight and differentiate the city's urban heritage and identity. As the groups came together to begin the design process, the planning team took time not only to describe the desired end product, but also to discuss the nature of collaboration and its impact on the creative process—both good (teamwork) and bad (resistance). The teams were given a project schedule and guidelines to help them focus on the task at hand. Each team was asked to assign its members specific roles (timekeeper, scribe, spokesperson, etc.) and a representative of the city's Gateway program offered a presentation detailing the design challenges posed by the project.

Not surprisingly, given the diverse nature of the groups, teams responded to the project challenge in a wide variety of ways. However, both the planning team and the student observers made some interesting common observations:

- A team needed people not only from different disciplines, but also with different personalities to work collaboratively. It was noted that the team with the most similar personality types and skill sets had the most difficult time in developing a common design scheme.
- At times, flexibility in roles, such as changing leaders at different phases of the design process, proved beneficial to the design process.
- Imposing a rigid schedule may have had a negative effect, causing teams to truncate the conceptual phase of design and make decisions prematurely.
- Requiring teams to develop a Mission Statement helped them to focus more effectively on a common approach.
- Successful collaboration did not appear to be something that happened by accident. Those teams that subsumed the product to the process—that is, they consciously followed guidelines and were good active listeners—developed a product that was equal, if not superior, to those groups whose participants acted more independently, as evaluated by the participants themselves.

While not a scientific test, the bottom line, according to the planning team, is that "getting the right group together and working with set guidelines, can be invigorating and produce a whole that is greater than the sum of its parts."[2]

In a Visioning Workshop, it's also important that, for the time being, all the participants working together share equal footing and are bound by a common goal, which is achieving a vision for the organization or project at hand. Status is banished. The entire organization is going to be responsible for delivering the new experiences that manifest the vision. Everybody knows that each one owns a piece of the dream. As I said before, if they have a say in it, they're more likely to make it happen.

BEFORE THE VISIONING WORKSHOP BEGINS

The Visioning Workshop, which I describe below, is the centerpiece of the Dream phase. But there is one step that must be taken first—a presentation of the results of the Discover phase.

Recall that the Discover phase captures a snapshot of where your organization is now. What does the condition of your 4Ps say about how your customers and other stakeholders are experiencing your company? During this brief presentation, typically held at the beginning of a Visioning Workshop, the facilitator presents the group with evidence of how your operation currently works—or doesn't—in terms of delivering the kinds of experiences you aspire to deliver to your customers, clients, employees, members, students, guests, patients—whomever your stakeholders are. Additionally, any competitive analysis, benchmarking, or other research completed during the Discover phase typically is presented to workshop participants at this point, to get them to better understand where the organization is before determining where it wants or needs to go.

This brief interlude helps galvanize in the participants' minds how important the rest of this process is in helping them bring their organization up to its full potential.

THE PURPOSES OF VISIONING WORKSHOPS

There are two distinctly different Visioning Workshops in terms of the desired outcome—the Organizational Visioning Workshop and the Project Visioning Workshop. Many of the session components are the same, but their purposes and outcomes are different. In an Organizational Visioning Workshop, the purpose and outcome is the development of a Vision Statement, which will guide all organizational activities and decisions and form the basis of the organization's strategic plan. In a Project Visioning Workshop, the purpose and outcome is the development of a vision for a specific project—a new Web site, building, training program, advertising campaign, and so on, and to use that vision to guide the design of the new project in an integrated way.

Let's look at the Organizational Visioning Workshop first. If you are launching a new organization or significantly redesigning the *raison d'etre* of your organization, the Organizational Visioning Workshop is where you want to begin. The Organizational Visioning Workshop will help you identify the essential elements of your enterprise—those that are timeless and those that change with the times. This type of session is critical when there's a new enterprise being created, or the existing business or organization is undergoing such a major transformation that it's time to revisit the entire entity as if starting from scratch. Other times at which an Organizational Visioning Workshop would be very useful include the following:

- There is a transition in power that is causing a cultural shake-up internally.
- There is a new mandate for the organization to identify how it is authentically different from its competition so it can better stand out and become more competitive in the marketplace.
- The organization has been experiencing extremely fast growth, and the leaders see that the organization is moving quickly away from its original vision and toward a new position in the marketplace or industry.
- The business is just getting started and needs to have a road map for its future success.
- There is a new alliance of different companies for a shared goal.
- The company is experiencing a new and very impactful market development that has the potential to change everything about the organization and how it operates.
- The industry within which the organization operates is experiencing significant changes.
- The company identifies new opportunities to leverage, which will have a significant impact on the organization.

This process, inspired by the work of business consultants Dick Cross and Jane LaPoint, helps you come to an understanding of who you are as framed by your most fundamental truth about your enterprise—your Vision Statement, which is organized around two concepts: DNA and Drivers of Progress.

DNA

Similar to human DNA, these are ideas and tenets that are *born* with the organization; for truly successful, long-standing businesses, they remain with the organization for life. Although, as with human DNA, some evolutionary refinement can occur over time.

The DNA of any Vision Statement serves as an anchor for your company, providing stability and focus, especially during difficult times. The DNA of any organization includes its Core Beliefs and Values (the ideals in which it deeply believes) and its Purpose (the reason the organization exists).

Drivers of Progress

These are the organizational tenets and focus that *must* change over time, because the marketplace constantly changes, requiring new ideas and actions to meet new marketplace demands. The Drivers of Progress include an organization's Mission Statement (those goals that an organization will accomplish during a set period of time) and a Tangible Image (a description of what life will be like once an organization achieves its mission).

A Project Visioning Workshop may or may not involve the development of an entirely new vision for the organization itself. But when you are able to interlace your Project Vision, not for a new or hugely revised organization, but for a new building, a new advertising campaign, or a new customer experience, with the essential values and components of your new or existing Organizational Vision, you will achieve a stronger, better supported project that stands the best opportunity to be made manifest.

While you may have only a very limited number of opportunities to go through an Organizational Visioning process, you may have multiple opportunities to conduct Project Visioning Workshops throughout your career or the lifespan of your business. When you experience the full value of the process, you will want to apply it as frequently as possible, whether it's for a new building or a new operational initiative, a new company brochure, or a new product or service. Or perhaps a new surge in hiring, when a transformation in your business means that you need to be more specific about the kinds of people and personalities you bring onboard. Projects typically are less complex than a complete organizational transformation. But whatever the project may be, if it has the potential to dramatically change the experience that your stakeholders will have with your company, you will want to make it consistent with your larger overall Organizational Vision and Mission Statement.

THE VISIONING WORKSHOP

This is the time for participants to develop their own big, unified, and authentic vision through a series of facilitated exercises designed to appeal to the variety of learning and communication styles of the participants. Introverts, for instance, who do their thinking in the privacy of their own minds, are often less comfortable than their extroverted counterparts in sharing their thoughts, ideas and feelings with a large group. Some people learn by doing. For others, reading or writing is the way they get the most from a learning experience. All voices deserve to be heard, and all learning and communication styles need to be honored to get the most out of a Visioning Workshop.

Additionally, each exercise is designed to build on the common understanding that the entire group has achieved during the previous exercise. Not only is the process collaborative, but its iterative nature also results in better ideas through the constant refinement that happens when people share their ideas with one another.

CREATING AN ORGANIZATIONAL VISION

The workshop begins with the facilitator welcoming the participants, reviewing the workshop purpose and goals, and providing a general outline of the day. It's important that the facilitator not share the specific details of any of the following exercises, which are designed to appeal to a wide variety of people and the different ways that we think, learn, and communicate. Therefore, while some of the exercises may not appeal to or be comfortable for everyone in group, there is a purpose to all of them that will become apparent during the course of the day.

Metaphoria

What people find difficult to express in words often can be more easily expressed with pictures. As a result, Metaphoria is one of the most popular and effective exercises in the Visioning Workshop. This initial exercise is important as it helps address any current concerns or issues about the organization in a safe and nonthreatening manner through the use of images. Often, if sensitive or politically charged issues are not dealt with or acknowledged, they could get in the way of or jeopardize the creation and implementation of a new and better experience for all.

During this first exercise, a series of 50 or more very diverse images are posted on a wall. The images range from a photo of a truck stuck in the branches of a tree, to a group of hikers scaling a mountain top. The facilitator asks a question of the group depending upon the desired outcome of the workshop. In an Organizational Visioning Workshop, for example, the question is, "If our current organization were a metaphorical image, which one would we select to represent the current state of our organization?" Each participant small group then selects an image that represents the current state of their organization and shares it with the larger group, explaining why the small group chose that particular image.

Metaphorical images help people to more easily express thoughts and ideas.
Photo by Digital Vision/Media Bakery.

Photo © Kahler Slater, Inc.

In one session with a higher education client group, for example, one small group chose a photograph of a fisherman attempting to unravel what looks like a hopelessly tangled web of fishing line and nets. "I chose this image because I feel as if we're in a real mess right now," said one administrator who represented her group. "I love this school, but I think we're all moving in different directions without a common goal. And we're at cross purposes rather than working together." Within her group and, indeed, throughout the room, heads nodded slowly and silently in agreement.

Sometimes, groups choose images and describe ideas that are not in concert with one another, which is one reason why this exercise is presented early in the session. The facilitator's job then, before moving forward, is to work with the group to verbally explore any disconnects or misperceptions of the group at this highest level. It's difficult, if not impossible, to move forward into a new future Organizational Vision if key stakeholders within the organization can't even agree about where they're starting from! At the completion of this exercise, the facilitator works with the overall group to select one image which best expresses the collective thoughts and feelings of the entire group as to their current state.

Determining the DNA: Core Beliefs and Values and Purpose

Next, after breaking into new small groups, the participants will be asked to work together to develop a list of what they believe to be the organization's most important Core Beliefs and Values. These are the words that express the desired attitudes and behaviors of everyone who works within the organization.

The groups are asked to finish the following sentence: "At our organization, we believe deeply in. . . ." Other questions asked by the facilitator to prompt discussion include: "How do we want our staff to treat one another? How do we want our staff to behave, day in and day out? How do we want our staff to treat customers and visitors? For what qualities is our organization known, and how do we want to be known?"

The values that this exercise—and, indeed, the entire Organizational Visioning Workshop—elicit are intended to be a balance between reality and aspiration. You'll want the group to respond with answers to these questions in a way that reflects current reality. But if the current reality is something that the organization wants and has the capacity to improve upon, then it should aim higher, and participants should offer ideas that stretch the organization toward something better. This is especially important in terms of developing a vision that is authentic.

After an initial brainstorming of 10 minutes, each group will be asked to cull their longer list to 5 to 7 of the top Core Beliefs and Values, and share them with the entire, larger group. The facilitator keeps a running list of the values, noting how many times a single value is mentioned by a group. At the end of the exercise, the group agrees to the top five to seven Core Beliefs and Values.

The Core Beliefs and Values are one key element of the new Vision Statement that should resonate with everyone. So, if, for instance, the Vision Statement includes a Core Belief and Value of *honesty*, but some staff believe that current organizational practices or people aren't in keeping with this value, then the question that must be answered before the Vision Statement can or will be embraced by all is: "If we aren't as honest as we should be now, does the organization have the capacity and the will to become more honest over time?" If the answer is *no*, then the leaders have some work to do before they finalize their Vision Statement.

Values Auction

It's not all that uncommon for a group, especially a large group, to fail to reach consensus during this exercise. To help them to do so quickly, the facilitator could hold a Values Auction.

To begin, the facilitator distributes the same amount of play money to each participant or small group. The list of all Core Beliefs and Values are then displayed for all to see, and are *auctioned* off, one by one, to the participants or small groups. Participants can spend all of their money on one value. Or they can team up and pool their money with other participants or small groups to buy a particular value. They also can choose to keep all their money (indicating through their lack of interaction that the stated values mean very little to them in the first place, or aren't seen as authentic or actionable).

The discussion that ensues among participants during the course of the auction is usually quite telling with regard to which values seem the most *real,* and which don't. By the end of the auction, the five to seven Core Beliefs and Values that sell for the most money are identified as the most important to the group. Again, these should later be shared across the organization, and even shared with customers or other stakeholders, to see whether they hold up as true and authentic to the existing or future organization.

Purpose Statement

The next step in the Organizational Visioning Workshop is to develop a Purpose Statement. After organizing into new small groups, participants are asked to finish another statement, this one describing their organization's fundamental reason for being. The statement, "We exist to . . ." should be finished in as direct and succinct manner as possible. To encourage discussion, the facilitator asks the groups to consider the following questions:

- What is it that you're passionate about?
- What is the essential value your organization brings to the marketplace?
- What is it about your organization that gets you out of bed in the morning, and makes you want to work here?
- What is it that you do on a qualitative level?
- How does what you do at its essential core positively affect you, your world, your staff, and the marketplace you serve?

After a 15-minute brainstorming period, each group is asked to refine their ideas into one sentence. The sentence should be factual, but also serve as an inspiration for your organization. Remember, the Core Beliefs and Values and the Purpose are the part of the Vision Statement that serves as the DNA of an organization. As such, for a new organization, it should stand the test of time. And for those organizations undergoing a reorganization, or those which have never had a Vision Statement during the course of their organizational lives, the Core Beliefs and Values and Purpose Statement should be as true today and into the future as it was when the organization was founded—unless, of course, the DNA is flawed (and, thus, shouldn't serve as the bedrock of the organization) and new DNA is required.

The facilitator will call for group report-backs, and will work with the entire group to reach consensus on the development of a Purpose Statement that is shared by all.

DEVELOPING THE DRIVERS OF PROGRESS: MISSION AND TANGIBLE IMAGE

You'll recall that a Vision Statement involves two parts: the DNA, which changes very little, if at all through the years; and the Drivers of Progress, which are intended to change in response to the needs of your employees and customers.

The facilitator will ask participants (who are now in new small groups) to define several Mission Statements, or those ideas and activities which help an organization focus its efforts in order to achieve its Purpose and authentically live its Core Beliefs and Values. The Mission Statements will form the basis of the road map or strategic plan to get the organization to its desired future. Some questions that prompt discussion during this exercise include:

- What is it that you wish to accomplish, given your Purpose?
- How will you achieve your Purpose?

It's also helpful to provide the group with examples of the Mission Statements of other companies or organizations. Google's Mission Statement, for example, is "to organize the world's information and make it universally accessible and useful." Walmart's is "to help people save money so they can live better." These statements should be succinct, and need not get bogged down in the detail of how you'll accomplish your mission. That's what an organization's strategic plan is for, with each Mission Statement forming the basis for the organization's future strategies and tactics. Mission Statements should be measureable, or have the potential to be measured, even if you're not sure at this point what the measurement should or could be. Additionally, Mission Statements should be something staff members are able to visualize.

Using the framework of the 4Ps is a great place for each group to start developing the five to seven Mission Statements they'll be asked to present after an hour or so of discussion. For example, given the newly defined Core Beliefs and Values of the organization, and its Purpose (or reason for existing), what kind of Perception does the organization need to have in order to be true to its DNA? What kind of People does it need to hire, and how should they be trained to deliver on the organization's Purpose in a way that is consistent with the Core Beliefs and Values? Are there new Products and/or Services that are required in order to achieve the organizational Purpose, or are there offerings that need to be refined or eliminated from the organization? Finally, is the Place where work gets done in keeping with and supportive of the DNA of the organization?

During report-backs, the facilitator will note common themes and ideas that surface. Groups are encouraged to challenge one another during report-backs, to ask questions and provide feedback. In the end, a set of five to seven (those magic numbers again!) Mission Statements will emerge, and serve as the foundation for the strategic and tactical business and operational plans to come.

Finally, participants will turn their attention to developing a Tangible Image. This is a crucial step in the development of an Organizational Vision Statement, and in our experience, it's one which, unfortunately, far too many organizations skip. Research shows that what gets measured gets done, which is one reason why Mission Statements must be measureable. But research also shows that people who have a solid picture in their minds of what will happen when they achieve their goals are more likely to get there. Think of the Olympic athlete who, through each grueling workout, gets through the pain by imagining herself on the trophy stand with a gold medal around her neck. Or the entrepreneur who imagines what life will be like when his new invention hits the market. These mental images are critical in helping people to imagine a better future—one that is specific, exciting and achievable, not vague, unknown, frightening, and unreachable. The Tangible Image statements are what inspire staff, and serve to provide focus, motivation and reassurance when times are tough.

New small groups will be asked to develop a Tangible Image, or those five to seven statements that specifically describe what life will be like when the organization achieves its mission to live out its Purpose in a way that's consistent with its Core Beliefs and Values. Some questions to facilitate this discussion include:

- What experiences do you want your staff to have once you've reached your goals?
- What experiences do you want your customers or other stakeholders of your organization to have once you've reached your goals?

As with the Mission Statement development, each small group will report back their ideas, with the facilitator encouraging feedback and discussion among the groups. This exercise can last anywhere from 45 minutes to 2 hours, depending upon how close the group is to achieving consensus as to the final list of five to seven statements.

We're coming to the close of an Organizational Visioning Workshop. But remember Metaphoria (the metaphorical image exercise we described earlier in this chapter), which kicks off an Organizational Visioning workshop? At the end of this kind of workshop, we replay the Metaphoria exercise. But this time, we ask participants to select an image that represents the organization *in the future,* as represented by the Tangible Image, after it has achieved its collective Vision Statement as articulated and developed during the workshop. This exercise, with its aspirational result, offers hope to sometimes frustrated or impatient leaders and staff who want everyone in the organization to understand and embrace their vision—if they could only articulate exactly what that vision really is.

One popular image often selected during this final exercise is of a basket of white eggs, with one golden egg in the middle—which can evoke the goal of marketplace differentiation or of a one-of-a-kind value or success. Other popular images emphasize the themes of people working together, such as putting a hang glider into the air or groups scaling a mountain together. It doesn't matter so much what the image is as long as the entire group interprets it in the same way. The image, even more than the words used to describe it, will serve as the organization's *true north,* or a kind of visual and emotional shorthand reminder of the vision achieved long after the session is over. In six months or even a year later, when there's a crisis that requires a

Metaphorical images serve as a visual reminder of an organization's *true north*.
Photo © Kahler Slater, Inc.

difficult choice or change in behavior, the group can return to that image and remind themselves what it stands for, and then make their decision in concert with the values and vision represented by that image. Ending an Organizational Visioning Workshop on this note is inspirational and satisfying for all participants.

After the session, the group is encouraged to develop a communications plan to share the newly created Vision Statement with all of their staff. This can be achieved in a variety of ways. One client (a small business owner) printed out the Vision Statement developed by his leadership team, and held small group meetings with all employees over the course of two days to obtain feedback from his staff. One company took a similar approach, but posted the printed Vision Statement in the lunchrooms of its offices, along with providing sticky notes and pens, encouraging employees to add their remarks or make edits to the documents (anonymously or not). If you're truly interested in finalizing a Vision Statement that rings true, one which is your authentic organizational thumbprint that belongs to your company and your company alone, then all stakeholders need a chance to weigh in with their opinions and reactions. Again, those who own it are more likely to believe it, and work to achieve it.

Once you're satisfied with your Vision Statement, and have adjusted it according to the feedback you receive, it will serve as your foundation for strategic planning (as previously noted), as well as a filter for all decision making throughout your organization. It should also become a part of your employee review and goal-setting process, and be used as a guide for budgeting—determining what the organization values and will resource, and what it won't. In short, the Vision Statement serves as an organization's authentic roadmap for its future success.

THE PROJECT VISIONING WORKSHOP

When the outcome of a workshop is a *project* (a new Web site, service offering, building, operational procedure, and so forth) rather than a new Organizational Vision Statement, we use many of the same small group processes and exercises, but we often ask slightly different questions of the participants. For instance, in using the Metaphoria exercise to kick off a Project Visioning Workshop, we ask a more future-oriented question: "In the future, when we've achieved all of our goals for this project, it will be like. . . ." Again, participants are asked to think about how they might best complete this sentence and which metaphorical image they'd select that best represents their answers.

When conducting the Metaphoria exercise for a replacement hospital for Martha Jefferson Hospital (Charlottesville, Virginia), President and CEO James Haden held up a picture of a crocheted afghan slung over the back of a rocking chair on the porch of a neat, white clapboard house to illustrate his group's ideas for a new hospital addition. In explaining the image the group selected, he said that he in particular was drawn to the image because, like the rest of his group, he wanted patients to feel safe, loved, and at home in the new hospital environment—an experience that had yet to be designed. The image evoked the feelings of being welcomed and comfortable, which were the focus he and his team desired for the new hospital. "We originally chose the image of a pianist sitting at a grand piano, because it represented excellence to us. But then we decided that excellence should be a given in any hospital setting," he said.

For some clients, the vision of the future success of their project is very specific and apparent to them. This exercise offers the opportunity for them to more easily translate their vision to those who will help them to achieve it. For instance, when Robert Redford and his Sundance team were working on the design for a new independent cinema experience, Redford described his idea of success for the new, yet to be designed, theater, restaurant, bar, coffee shop, retail store, and community gathering space as expressing a kind of *rough elegance*. To him, these words perfectly captured the essence of the new experience and environment he wanted to create: an experience that would be comfortable, timeless, and look good, but not be formal or over-done. To him, these two words also were very much in keeping with the well-established essence of the Sundance brand. Having built this well-known brand over time, Redford wanted to ensure that this new prototype project would be in sync with it. The client and experience design team set-

The Sundance 608 theater corridor features rough birch trees highlighted with soft lighting, creating an elegant experience. *Photo © Todd Dacquisto.*

tled on the image of a worn jean jacket to symbolize the words Redford chose to sum up his vision. This image and the words offered by Redford to describe his thoughts were used by the team to guide all design decisions during the course of the project.

Project Drivers

The next exercise in a Project Visioning Workshop helps participants identify specific characteristics of what success will look like when their newly stated Project Vision (along with the metaphorical image they've chosen to represent it) is actually made manifest. All of us use these *Project Drivers* regularly in our day-to-day lives. Take buying a car, for instance. Before we venture out to the car lots, we most likely know which makes we are interested in; whether we want manual or automatic transmission; what model we want (SUV? Convertible? Coupe?). What year. Perhaps even what color. These are all filters through which we pass the many options before us and then make our ultimate determination as to whether our choice was a successful one. And knowing what we want at the outset helps us make better decisions much more quickly.

Likewise, while working toward achieving a Project Vision, a prioritized list of Project Drivers focuses organizational energies on those ideas or measures of success that the group collectively believes will get them to their desired future faster and better than all the rest.

Just as the Metaphoria exercise is designed to appeal to those participants who are visionary, big picture kinds of folks, Picture Success, or the exercise that identifies specific Project Drivers, is designed to appeal to the more practical, analytical people in the group who need tactical metrics to achieve success.

After organizing into new groups, the facilitator begins with a visualization exercise. The groups are asked to imagine that the project at hand is complete, and that it has met, and perhaps even exceeded, the goal of making manifest its intended Project Vision. If, for example, the new project experience being designed involves a new facility, the facilitator will ask the group to imagine that they're at the ribbon-cutting ceremony for the new building, and that everyone is happy with the result. The facilitator might ask the group to imagine who is there, and what they're saying that makes the experience such a success. The idea is to paint a vivid and rich image of the new experience and to identify exactly what makes it so successful. Once the group has this picture of success firmly established in their minds' eyes, the participants are asked to finish this sentence: "In the future when we've achieved our Project Vision, this new experience will be a success when . . ."

Project Drivers serve as filters for decision making. *Photo © Kahler Slater, Inc.*

To give the groups a running start on some completion ideas, the facilitator might toss out these phrases:

- "It looks . . ."
- "It seems . . ."
- "We have . . ."
- "We no longer have . . ."
- "We have plenty of . . ."
- "I am able to . . ."
- "The community can . . ."
- "Our team can . . ."
- "My boss/team/mom would think . . ."

The groups should brainstorm all the possible endings to the sentence. They're aiming for quantity at this stage of the exercise, not quality. After 10 to 15 minutes, the facilitator then assigns each group the task of picking five to seven of the best answers from the lists of possible ideas that have been generated. A representative from each group presents to the entire room what his or her team has come up with. (If you have a sense of which group might be most likely to present the most innovative answers, have that group present first. That way that group will raise the bar for the rest of the participants who follow.)

Write down all the answers, noting how many of them are duplicate answers so as to assess the collective importance of these duplicates to the larger group. And then have the entire group pick the top five to seven answers as their final Project Drivers—those characteristics that will help them make choices along the way to achieve their collective Project Vision and achieve success. Because they selected them, they will own them emotionally. You also will discover that the final grouping of drivers usually correlate with the 4Ps. If not, then the facilitator can use the 4Ps to prompt further review of and discussion about the proposed Project Drivers.

For example, the marketing and communications agency Cramer-Krasselt developed the following Project Vision and Drivers to guide the design for its new office:

PROJECT VISION

When we are in our new office, and working in a way that best expresses our brand, our culture, and our values, it will be like a Noguchi table. A modern classic that is playful, creative, and cool—never trendy. It's where people come together to collaborate. It's beautiful, accessible, and comfortable. It expresses energy and inspires confidence.

Selected metaphorical image–a Noguchi coffee table. *Courtesy of Hermann Miller, Inc.* © *The Isamu Noguchi Foundation and Garden Museum, New York.*

PROJECT DRIVERS

This project will be a success when . . .

- It allows us to work together effectively with no barriers.
- It attracts talent and becomes the house where "all the kids want to play."
- It inspires confidence, keeps us current, and challenges people to do their best and feel good about it.
- It's a place that gives us a sense of pride and becomes a destination for bringing in new prospects.
- It's a place that asks all who enter to challenge the status quo and do better than before.

An international beverage company, with operations in the United States and Puerto Rico, developed this Project Vision and Project Drivers to set the stage for its new Chicago marketing office, which was intended to serve as a potential prototype for the overhaul of its dated corporate headquarters:

PROJECT VISION

When we are fully achieving our vision, we will be bringing together our individual strengths and passions in a way that is seamless, challenging, fun, and, in the end, producing great results. Our competition will fear us. And our customers will love us for enhancing the simple pleasures of their lives.

Selected metaphorical image–a couple passionately engaged in dancing the tango. © *iStockphoto.com/1001nights.*

PROJECT DRIVERS

This project will be a success when . . .

- We are using state-of-the-art technology to its full capacity which provides for seamless communication.
- People feel the passion that we have for the business.
- It reflects that we're a progressive company that cares about its people.
- People are inspired and visually stimulated by the space.
- We see improved marketing output.
- The Chicago office inspires change in terms of:
  - Collaboration.
  - Model of content/contact integration.
  - Passion/creativity.
  - Work/life balance.
  - Work habits not restricted.
- It attracts and retains top talent and resources to work at our company, no matter what the location.
- People from other offices want to go there for meetings.
- People from other offices want to upgrade their workplace to be like Chicago.
- You can walk in and immediately feel the energy.
- Any visitor will immediately know it's our company.
- The space offers maximum flexibility.
- The space displays our proud history and cultural aspirations.

While this exercise seems fairly straightforward, it's not unusual for participants to struggle to reach consensus. In these instances, the facilitator can *force* the cream to rise to the top by asking which ideas are absolutely required to achieve the stated Project Vision—in other words, if we don't do "X" we simply will not be able to achieve our Project Vision, no matter what else we choose to do. An alternative approach is to write down all the drivers on large sheets of paper posted on the walls. The facilitator then gives participants five dots each, instructing them to use their dots to vote for the drivers that they believe are the most critical to achieve the Project Vision. Participants can spend all five dots any way that they want to. They can spend them all on one driver. They can form alliances with other participants in favor of certain drivers and not others. Once the dots have been placed next to the selected driver(s), the facilitator identifies the top five to seven vote getters and confirms with the participants that those are the drivers that are the most important to them.

Another fun and effective exercise that is used in large group decision making that appeals particularly to the kinesthetic learner, or those who learn best by using their bodies in the process of learning or communicating, is the Barn Dance. This is also a particularly good exercise to do after lunch, or anytime when the energy of the group needs a boost.

The facilitator writes down all the Project Drivers on small pieces of paper and puts them in a bag (making sure there are the same number of Project Drivers as there are people in the large group). Similar Project Drivers may be combined, or duplicates of those drivers that seem redundant should be eliminated. Each person selects a driver out of the bag—making certain that no one has selected a driver that they came up with themselves, to avoid anyone having a sense of personal ownership of any particular Project Driver.

Start some energetic music—square dancing tunes work with the Barn Dance theme. When your participants hear the music playing, they should move around the room, mingling with each other one-on-one, even do-si-do'ing or swinging partners—assuming, of course, that they can square dance. Whatever they're doing, they should be interacting in ever-changing pairs of two.

After 10 to 15 seconds, stop the music and have the current sets of pairs compare drivers and assign point values to them. To do so, they must answer the question: "Which of these two drivers is better, or is better suited, to help us realize our vision?" There is only one winner in each pairing, and if the winning driver is deemed to be *significantly* better than the other, it gets 100 points. If the winning driver is only slightly better than the other, it gets 50 points. The loser, of course, gets 0 points in either case. Participants write the total score on the back of the winning driver.

Each round of voting should take no more than 30 seconds, so the assessment is based purely upon the quick gut reaction of each participant. After the voting and assigning of points is complete, the couple should exchange drivers. Again, this ensures that no one person gets too attached to a single driver. It also protects against the unfair advantage that might be had by any super salespeople in the group who can more easily *sell* one particular driver to whomever they meet up with. (You know the type—the guy who could talk a dog off a meat truck.)

Start the music again. Make sure that participants have a new partner for every round. Continue the rounds until the group runs out of new partners (or you simply can't stand to hear any more square dancing music). By the end of the exercise, add up all of the scores to determine the top-graded drivers as the most valuable drivers as determined by the entire group.

A Day in the Life™

Armed with a Project Vision for the future, and Project Drivers that serve as filters for all of the creative ideas to come, the next exercise is to imagine what it will be like to be a customer, client, student, patient, or any other critical stakeholder in your organization once you've made manifest your vision. The large group is once again organized into new teams of five to seven participants each. Each group is asked to select a photograph and corresponding biography of a *typical* stakeholder for whom the organization wants to create an ideal experience based upon the stated Project Vision and Project Drivers. Each biography offers a different demographic and psychographic profile of a stakeholder and describes information appropriate to the experience being designed. The information can include the individual's family situation, likes and dislikes, hobbies, educational background, as well as the stakeholder's relationship to the organization. For example, in the case of designing a better experience for a student at a local community college, the biography might read something like the example on the top of page 102.

Participants are then asked to imagine that it is sometime in the future and that the organization has fully achieved its Project Vision and all related goals. The organization has become what it has intended to be, in every area as defined by the Project Drivers and represented by the 4Ps. The task at hand at this point is to imagine how the person whose biography they've selected will experience the transformed organization in terms of all 4Ps during an ideal day: What's the person's Perception of the organization? How do the People who work here treat him? What brings the person here? How does the person physically get here? When the person arrives, what happens then? What ideal Product is offered or Service is delivered? What does the Place where all of this happens ideally look like, and how does it function? All 4Ps are considered at the same time so that they can be purposely designed in an integrated fashion, because as I've previously noted, even small disconnects between any of the 4Ps can negatively impact the entire experience.

Participants are encouraged to think about an *ideal* experience they're creating in a multisensory manner. What does the person see, hear, smell, taste, and touch during this ideal experience? With whom does this person interact during this experience and how does this interaction make the person feel? And on it goes, with participants creating ideal and authentic total experiences that, informed by the Project Drivers, become a manifestation of the fully realized Project Vision at every level, and in every way.

As these ideal experiences are being designed, participants are asked to capture the elements of their stories in the way best suited to them. Magazines, scissors, colored pencils, and markers are available for the "artists" in the group to tell their stories using graphics and images. Pens, pads of paper, and diaries

Photo by Photodisc/Media Bakery.

Who Am I?

Name:	Jeff Decker
Personal Information:	19 years old, Male, Caucasian, Single
Area of study:	Accounting Assistant
Educational background:	GED
Campus attending:	Watertown

Vital statistics: Jeff has always been good at math, so he thought he'd give the accounting assistants program a try. It was one of the programs he could take at the Watertown campus so he wouldn't have to travel so much. Although he was worried about taking such a challenging program after dropping out of high school two years ago, he's been surprised that he's been able to keep up. The school is even smaller than his high school, which has helped. He's even surprised his family by maintaining a GPA of 3.7.

Frame of mind: He likes the closeness of the campus, he just wishes there was more here. It kind of stinks that he has to run home or go out for lunch since there's nothing on campus but vending machines. He'd much rather spend that time studying. One of his classes is at the high school, which feels kind of odd. In some ways, it's like he never left. Working toward a degree seems to have given him a goal he feels he can achieve.

are available for those who express themselves through the written word. (One team from an international staffing company actually expressed the story and ideal experiences they designed for the person whose biography they chose through a short modern dance performance. And it successfully conveyed the meaning and experiences they wanted to share with the entire group!)

Once participants have a complete idea of what it's like to be their selected stakeholder, they are then challenged to apply the particulars of the new Project Vision that they developed at the very beginning of the workshop to the ideal experience that this person might have with the organization. How might technology (both current and future, real and imagined) impact that ideal experience they're designing? Or how might something as mundane (or potentially threatening) as the weather dramatically impact an experience? What are all the elements of the ideal total experience, and how might variables in these stakeholders' lives influence the way they experience the authenticity of the organization?

The participants answer these questions through stories. And the storytelling makes the experience real. At the end of the Day in the Life exercise, the groups tell their stories through the perspective of the stakeholders they selected. This allows all involved in the session the opportunity to see and hear how the future Project Vision is interpreted by and applied to a variety of stakeholders, as represented by the biographies. The act of telling stories helps determine whether the entire group is on the same page, and it inspires additional creative thinking through the sharing of new ideas.

No idea is too weird to be considered, as this often leads to other ideas that can be more easily implemented. For instance, during a workshop with a community college client, one group shared that in their ideal Day in the Life experience, people on campus moved to and fro on moving sidewalks. While this idea wasn't very practical for a number of reasons, it did elicit a discussion about the difficulty students had in dodging traffic to get to class at this commuter college, which led to real solutions for enhancing pedestrian safety and mobility.

These report-back sessions also can be quite emotional. One visionary leader, who had been professionally and personally frustrated with the way in which health care was delivered to her daughter during the birth of her first child, struggled to fight back tears as she shared with the rest of the workshop participants the ideal experience story of the stakeholder whom her group chose. Not surprisingly, the ideal experience story that her group created was in direct contrast to her daughter's personal and terrible experience. At the end of the day, she whispered to the experience design facilitator, "Please don't leave me until we can make this new experience happen."

Sharing the stories of desired ideal experiences makes them real. It answers the question of "what if we . . . ?" in a real and concrete manner, and allows participants to safely and creatively explore the future.

The Visioning Workshop, which occurs during the Dream phase of the process, offers a qualitative and emotionally compelling snapshot of what the ideal future might hold for an evolving or new organization and its key stakeholders. By the end of the workshop, participants will be equipped with the roadmap—a shared vision and, in the case of a Project Visioning Workshop,

Storytelling brings experiences to life. *Photo © Kahler Slater, Inc.*

Project Drivers—that will marshal and organize resources to get the organization to where it wants and needs to go.

These are all exercises that help participants transport themselves into the ideal future of what a successful project or company will look like when all the decisions are made according to the authentic vision for their organization and the ideal total experiences they want to deliver. They can dream wildly. They can imagine their ideal customers and all the different aspects of those lives that they will be able to serve through the work they do. They can identify the drivers that will help determine actions, decisions, and choices that they will continue to make to keep that solid dream intact and honored moving forward.

You and your team now know where you're going. And you know what you need to keep on course. You have begun to dream. Now your job is to determine how far you have to go and what actions you'll need to take to make the dream real.

Chapter 7

DEFINE—GETTING FROM HERE TO THERE

If you have built castles in the air, your work need not be lost; that is where they should be. Now, put the foundations under them.

Henry David Thoreau

© *iStockphoto.com/fotoyang.*

DEFINE

With Discover, you have learned what your current condition is. You have a fresh understanding of how your stakeholders experience your offerings right now. And, assuming you also did a competition audit and some benchmarking, you know how your organization stacks up against organizations similar to your own.

In the Dream phase, you took a trip into the future to paint a vivid picture of the kinds of stakeholders you want to serve and exactly what kinds of experiences you want them to have when they engage with you. By now, you are probably very inspired and excited to get on with the adventure of creating an organization that authentically represents everything you stand for. You're probably bursting to start designing all the specifics around the 4Ps and get your vision up and running as soon as possible.

But there's one more step before you enter the Design phase. And that's Define. If you are embarking on a major transformation of your organization, you already know that there are plenty of gaps between who you are now and who you want to be in the future. The Define phase is where you find out exactly what those gaps are and who will be assigned to close them.

Don't be demoralized by gaps. They're good to have. If after this Define phase you discover that you don't have very many gaps, if any at all, it's a sign that you may have set the Dream bar too low. Think of gaps as flashing signs: This way to the future of your own designing.

You should definitely have gaps. But you may not have the major gaps you think you do. In fact, the gaps that are really in the way of your designed future may be extremely simple to close. For example, a major national retailer discovered during its Dream phase that its employees wanted a more robust employee health and fitness program. Members of the HR department who participated in the Visioning Workshop responded after the workshop: "We're already doing it!" In fact, they had been quietly working on just such an employee program for a year, and were pleased to hear employees from throughout the company not only confirming their intent for the program during the workshop, but also making great suggestions for improvement prior to rolling it out. So the gap they identified wasn't that they didn't have a health and fitness program in the works for their employees. In fact, the gap they uncovered was a much more affordable challenge of simply improving the communication that the company was working on it, and letting employees know when they could expect implementation of the new program.

Often, the Define phase begins immediately after the Dream phase is concluded. The first step is to see how close your team thinks you are to having already achieved the dream according to the Project Drivers you have identified, and which you used as a guide toward creating ideal experiences for your key stakeholders. By now, the entire team will have a better and shared understanding of your vision, along with how the drivers will be used to achieve it. With the Dream phase team still assembled, post the Project Drivers so that everyone can see them at the same time. And then draw a line for each driver, representing a continuum, from 1 to 5. The 1 position represents the condition that the organization hasn't even begun to achieve anything related to that particular driver. And the 5 position represents that the vision as indicated by that driver has been fully realized.

During the Define phase, the gaps between where you are and where you want to be are identified. *Photo © Kahler Slater, Inc.*

Next, distribute adhesive dots to your participants (one dot per Project Driver) and ask them to place their dots on the continuums to indicate their opinions as to where the organization is on its way toward achieving each driver. This gap analysis will give you a sense of how unified the opinions are throughout the group. If you see that there is a wide distribution of the dots along the continuum (with one hospital client, the CEO put his dot on 5 while everyone else put their dots on 1; not a good sign), that's a gap in and of itself!

RETURNING TO THE SILOS

While the Dream phase brought everyone together without regard to organizational function, now is the time to send everyone back to their respective silos. Their assignment: We know what the dream is. Now what specifically do *you* need to do in order to help move the company toward the realization of that dream? What gaps have been identified that are yours, organizationally, to close? Using the 4Ps to map the discussion, each function or department will have very specific ideas as to what they must do to help achieve the dream. For instance:

Human Resources

Perception

Are the people who work for your company proud to be there? Does your organization have the reputation of being among the top employers in your field? Do your employees—what they wear, how they behave— appropriately reflect and communicate your authentic vision for the future? Are you sending the right messages in your talent recruiting and orientation materials about who you are, what you stand for, and how you work? Do your employees attract the kinds of customers your company wants to serve?

People

Does the organization have the right talent mix to support the new dream? Does HR need to source new populations of candidates to bring new skill sets onboard? Will the company have to shut down certain divisions? Will that mean a layoff in one business unit while HR recruits staff for other business units inside the organization? Should HR reach out to a different set of colleges to identify and recruit new generations of high performers that will help the organization to achieve its new vision?

Products and Services

What are the new products and services needed for your employees— training and professional development opportunities, comp and benefits programs, and so forth? Will they serve to attract and retain the kind of talent that will help the organization make the dream come true?

Place

Is your organization located in a safe or convenient part of town, where people can come to work without worry or distraction? Are the employees equipped with well-designed, functional, well-lit work spaces and ergonomic chairs and workspaces? Is the distribution of departments throughout the building conducive to the right kind of cross-silo brainstorming that leads to increased innovation? Does the place where work is done reflect the authentic vision for the organization's future?

Information Technology

Perception

Is your organization recognized as a great career opportunity for the marketplace's most talented technical experts? If IT is essential to customer service, do your customers have enough faith in your technical abilities to become external evangelists of your new dream?

People

Does the IT department have the latest technical knowledge to help move the company toward the new dream future? Do your IT people share the excitement of the new adventure and discovering how new technology will play a part in helping manifest the dream? Is the rest of the organization willing to learn new technological skills to help make the dream come true?

Products and Services

Is the organization willing to dedicate the necessary budget to ramp up the necessary IT capability in order to achieve the dream? Even if it means possibly taking money away from other pet projects? Do any of the new product or service ideas imagined during the Visioning Workshop require different/new technologies to bring them to market?

Place

Is your building physically capable of carrying the extra power load required by a ramped up IT capability? Does the interior layout of the building support new IT processes and/or equipment? If you're going to be offering new, high tech products and services to your customers and staff, is the place where this business is done modern, with the technological capability it needs to perform the necessary functions? Or does it look like a log cabin?

Financial

Perception

Does your organization have a solid reputation in the financial and banking community so that it can cover its expenses and provide the necessary funding for the dream?

People

Do your people have the financial resources they need to help contribute to achieving the dream? Do they have enough faith in your organization's financial health to stay loyal to your operation even as you go through the often painful early stages of organizational development? Can you afford to train, hire, and/or retain the type of employees you need to make your dream come true?

Products and Services

Can the financial side of the organization devise creative approaches to asset management so as to keep the operation stable while reaching for the new dream? Are you fiscally prepared to make the necessary investments to bring new products and services to market? Can you shut down certain product lines and services in order to ramp up for the dream set of offerings and give your people the time and resources to develop those new markets?

Place

Has the time come to sell and relocate? Would moving to a less expensive location free up the extra cash needed to make that new dream come true? Is there unused space in your building that you might be able to lease out? Would making your place more energy efficient free up more cash to invest in the dream for the future?

Research and Development

Perception

Is your company known as a place where creative minds can safely innovate, brainstorm, and even make mistakes without harming their careers?

People

Do you have the smartest, most creative, cutting-edge people on your team to create the knockout products and services you imagined for the future? Do your people attract other highly creative and innovative partners and potential job candidates?

Products and Services

How does your current set of offerings relate to your dream offerings? Is your dream a natural extension of what you're already doing? Or is this a revolutionary departure from your past? Do you have the necessary equipment to make the change?

Place

Is your company located in a hotbed of corporate creativity that is related to your line of business? For instance, if you're in software or biotechnology, are you located in one of the world's most prominent innovation incubators, such as Silicon Valley or North Carolina's Research Triangle? Is it important for you to be near top-ranked schools?

Customer Service

Perception

What are your customers saying about you? What is the response procedure when customers write with either complaints or compliments? Does this process need to be revised to align your customer service program and materials with your new dream? There is no universal right answer; just the correct answer that aligns with your new dream.

People

Does the new dream require a new customer-facing personality? Can you train your current staff to make the shift? What specific behaviors can your HR team identify that will help support the new dream's transformed customer service philosophy?

Products and Services

What will be your new customer-satisfaction philosophy? What return policy manifests the promises behind your new dream? How can you specifically tie the promises of your new dream to the dreams of your customers?

Place

Is your place of business easy to find? Is parking plentiful and safe? Are your locations sufficiently distributed throughout your market territory so that it's convenient for your customers to do business with you? Does your Web site offer clear directions to your headquarters? Do the directions lead the customer through attractive neighborhoods? Who are your neighbors? Are they companies with which you would be proud to be associated?

Distribution and Fulfillment

Perception

Is your packaging designed so that people know that the box is from your company without even having to look at the label? Does your package arrive at the customer's door looking crisp and new? Is there a sense of who you are around your package? Or is it just a humdrum plain box with collapsed corners and pinched edges?

People

Do you have the logistics and procurement experts necessary for this new reinvention? Do you need a new training program to make certain that everyone gets it right?

Products and Services

What new tracking software might you need to sustain the increased activity in the warehouse? Do you need newly designed packing boxes? Do you need to renegotiate your shipping contracts with delivery services? Can you set up a preferred customer account with your most active customers, so that they don't have to pay retail every time they purchase your products? If you ship online, what kind of security precautions must you have in place?

Place

If your company depends on trucking services, are you located conveniently to major interstate junctions? Do you need a new loading dock? Is it important that your location is convenient to a major airport?

These are just suggested questions. Your questions will probably be significantly different because no two organizations are alike. I went into this level of granular detail to demonstrate how any new dream can open up new challenges and opportunities in which every department in your company can get involved. The end result will be better designed, integrated and authentic total experiences for all your stakeholders that clearly differentiate your organization from your competitors.

The Define phase is a great opportunity to invite your entire organization to the task of discovering the details—large and small—that create gaps for you to close. In each of your departments, you have the experts you need to manifest your vision and make your dream come true.

Your Gaps Might Be Easier to Close than You Think

For organizations that want to design and deliver a thoroughly differentiated and authentic total customer experience, the Define phase might seem a bit discouraging. Its focus is on finding *all* the gaps that must be closed between who they are now and who they want to be when their dream is realized, which may seem daunting to some. However, the upside to the Define phase is that by identifying the gaps that must be closed, you may find that many of those gaps can be addressed in relatively minor, inexpensive, easy to handle, and extremely effective ways. So while you think you might need an expensive interior redesign, or even a new building, the Define phase may reveal a myriad of additional, much more manageable and even affordable ways in which gaps can—and must—be closed to achieve your dream. And closing those more accessible gaps might deliver the total experiences you want your customers to have more quickly than an expensive new training program, advertising campaign, or construction project.

For example, Flagler College, a small, private, liberal arts college in St. Augustine, Florida, discovered that advantage when it invited Performa Higher Education, a Kahler Slater subsidiary, to evaluate its college tour program for prospective students. Flagler's concerns centered on the overall welcome experience to the campus, which it had come to realize needed considerable improvement. Though the campus itself is dominated by a spectacular main building, which was once a luxurious resort, the college tours began and ended in a nondescript, cramped little house tucked unceremoniously in an obscure part of the property. Did that building set the right tone of welcome for the visitors? The Flagler administrators suspected that the answer would be no. So they invited Performa Higher Education to St. Augustine to offer an opinion.

Performa Higher Education accepted the invitation, but expanded its review far beyond simply focusing on questions concerning that one building. Using a combination Fresh Eyes Audit and Experience Audit process, Performa Higher Education looked at the entire prospective student tour experience using the 4P framework as a filter. Performa Higher Education began by reviewing the advance collateral materials sent to prospective students, as well as the intended and unintended messages sent to these same students via the Flagler Web site, and then went through the process just as visiting parents and prospective students might. In organizing its approach to the entire tour experience, Performa Higher Education broke the event down into these stages:

Prepare > Arrive > Engage > Connect > Extend

Flagler's Project Drivers were *personal, authentic, safe haven, character,* and *wonderment.* And so Performa Higher Education's main question was this: How did Flagler use each of these drivers to show off the school to its greatest advantage as being the kind of school where students would feel welcome and safe for four years while pursuing their academic goals? Did the touchpoints of the college tour experience integrate with each other to bring those drivers to life in the eyes of the prospective students and their parents?

Although the initial focus could have been on the actual building (Place) where the tours officially began, Performa Higher Education's ultimate set of recommendations extended far beyond the question of whether the building was a suitable center for the welcome experience. And many of its suggestions were immediately implementable at the same time as more complex and expensive decisions were being considered regarding creating a better physical home for the tour program. These are just a few examples of the recommendations that Performa Higher Education delivered to the college, each of which could be implemented almost immediately and at very low cost.

Perception

Performa Higher Education noticed that the Perception P offered perhaps the most opportunities to create an integrated total experience for visiting families. First of all, they suggested that the visitors not be called *visitors* at all. They are *guests*—a much more welcoming word that sets a tone for hospitality throughout the experience. The student tour guides became *student ambassadors.*

Throughout the campus tour experience and by reviewing the school's marketing materials (Web site, signage, correspondence, even doormats), the Performa Higher Education team spotted numerous easily closable gaps. There were, for instance, too many variations of Flagler College logos without strong, unifying elements, such as an established color palette. There were logos on the doormats, which seemed like a good idea at first. But do you really want people to wipe their feet on your logo? Even the student ambassador uniforms presented a small brand disconnect: The sky blue color had no relationship to the college's official school colors. Simply changing the colors of the ambassadors' shirts served as an inexpensive way to close a Perception gap.

People

Flagler recruited student ambassadors the way most colleges do—hiring them at the beginning of the academic year and concluding their employment at the arrival of summer. This convention created a few gaps in the quality of the tours, especially among the seniors, who might be distracted during their final college spring semester. Additionally, Flagler had so many student ambassadors that they each didn't have the chance to conduct more than a couple of tours a month, if that many. As a result, their delivery would become rusty between tours. Performa Higher Education recommended that Flagler appoint new tour ambassadors in January, so that freshmen students could have a chance at becoming tour ambassadors without having to wait until they were sophomores. That way, the seniors could be let off the hook in the spring, if they so desired. In addition, Performa Higher Education suggested a reduction in the number of ambassadors, allowing the average ambassador to lead more tours per month and to benefit from the additional experience (as well as to practice with the storyboarded new tour experience plan, which I describe next).

Products and Services

Like many other college tours, the Flagler tour had been very loosely organized, with student ambassadors showing guests generally what they wanted to show them. As a result, the Performa Higher Education audit team of four had four entirely different tours, seeing different buildings and hearing different information about the college—including information that really wasn't the most compelling to prospective students. High school seniors, for instance, may not be so interested in knowing how many volumes were contained in the school library. What they might prefer to hear is what campus life is really like for Flagler students. Performa Higher Education recommended that a full-time tour manager (or *campus guest program coordinator*) be hired and be dedicated to creating and managing a fully storyboarded tour that uniformly showed off the same buildings—with a special emphasis on locations with a *wow!* factor. But instead of simply parroting a canned script, the student ambassadors were encouraged to tell stories about their own authentic experiences on campus. The Performa Higher Education team also recommended that instead of holding a formal interview with a prospective student at the beginning of the tour, which is when counselors would explain the paperwork and application process and answer questions, the meeting should be held at the end of the tour. This way, guests would have the chance to actually bring questions to the meeting after having seen the campus and having heard the stories from the student ambassadors.

Place

St. Augustine is a lovely, historic city with a strong architectural appeal. One of the city's landmarks is the college's bell tower. These are assets that can be leveraged in the tour experience, even before the guests arrive on campus. For instance, there are two routes to the campus from the airport. The first is a more direct, faster route through a part of town that has seen better days. An alternative route takes guests through the attractive historic district and waterfront. Because the latter may take longer—especially if their cars get stuck behind a slow-moving horse and buggy—Flagler tour staff had been in the practice of directing guests through the more direct, less impressive parts of town. By resolving to route them through the historic district, guests have the chance to see St. Augustine at its absolute best. And the guest families can use the iconic bell tower as their destination target since it can be seen from almost everywhere in the historic district. Gap closed.

The team also recommended that instead of breezing visiting families through the impressive dining hall (one of the *wow!* locations), they should give the families the opportunity to actually enjoy a meal there. This way, prospective students and their families can experience the campus cuisine and have a chance to meet Flagler students, which contributes significantly to the authenticity of the experience.

When high-quality institutions and organizations such as Flagler College thrive for decades without going through a periodic Define phase, it's natural to expect their stakeholders' experiences to have slid away from their original intentions through the years. The happy surprise is that the Define gap

The Flagler College Bell Tower serves as a beacon for campus guests. *Photo © Kahler Slater, Inc.*

analysis process often reveals opportunities for minor tweaks and slight changes in behaviors, which can make a world of difference to both the organization and the experiences of its customers. A new building or redesign may or may not be necessary at the end of the day. But in the meantime, close the smaller gaps and you may find your organization coming a long way toward providing your customers with the integrated total experiences they desire. And when these highly valued total experiences are designed and delivered in an integrated manner that is authentic to your organization, they can't be replicated by your competitors.

Close the right gaps and your future as a highly differentiated organization with customers who are loyal beyond reason is right around the corner.

Chapter 8

DESIGN—MAKING CHOICES TO CLOSE THE GAPS

We live in a designed world, a world created by human thought, word, and deed. Language is the human design tool—dialogue the process. Everything from fashions to automobiles to school curriculum to health care practices to industrial production processes to organizations and communities—everything is designed in conversation.

Diana Whitney and Amanda Trosten-Bloom,
The Power of Appreciative Inquiry

Photo by Photodisc/Media Bakery.

DESIGN

When you think about design, especially in the context of a project that is visual, such as a brochure, a building, or a Web site, it's understandable that you might go immediately in the direction of aesthetics and form. What will the finished project *look* like? What is the color palette? What are the graphics? The textures? The lighting? The arrangement of furniture? What are the finishes? All are fair questions, if what you want is a pretty room or something attractive to hang on its wall. That is what *design* means to most people.

What if you're really reaching for a *total experience design* of, say, an entire organization—one that seamlessly delivers your product or service to your stakeholders? One that authentically differentiates your organization from your competitors? Then *design* means something different, especially in the context of the 5Ds. The Design phase is about more than just creating beautiful and functional spaces. It's about your team making purposeful choices about your entire organization, always keeping your vision and drivers in mind. So by making your design choices, addressing all 4Ps as you go, the result will be an integrated experience for all your stakeholders. And, in some cases, the result could change *everything* about what you do and how you do it.

When you approach design in the conventional and generic way, you start with a blank sheet of paper or whiteboard or new file on your computer monitor. The sky's the limit and your choices are seemingly endless, which might be tempting at first. But you may soon find yourself overwhelmed, confused, and perhaps utterly at the mercy of the prevailing influences of the person in power—in this case, the leader. But what happens if the leader changes midproject? Or if *you,* as the leader, change your mind in the middle of the night? Your people are vulnerable to too many capricious (not to mention extremely time-consuming and costly) changes. And if they're not unified by that previously agreed-upon vision, they are at risk of being pitted against one another as they compete for your favor and the money to pay for their piece of the vision.

This is not the case when you follow the 5Ds that will result in a total experience design. By the time you have entered the Design phase of the 5Ds, you already have your framework set in place. You and your team will know what your shared and authentic vision is for your enterprise, and you will have already identified the drivers that will help get your organization there (and keep it there regardless of what changes the future has in store for you and your stakeholders). The Design phase of the 5D process streamlines the time it takes to arrive at your final ideal outcome, saves immense amounts of time and money by eliminating shot-in-the-dark best guesses, and removes any kind of political power play between you and your team. And, to be perfectly frank, it also removes your own personal tastes and preferences as well. It is now up to your entire team to design your enterprise's future based on the vision and drivers that the entire group envisioned together in the Dream phase.

Going back to the 5D process that we've outlined so far: You know what your vision is for your enterprise. You know what your drivers are. And now, since you've just completed the Define phase, you know what your gaps are. The Design phase of the 5Ds is all about designing the specific strategies that will close those gaps.

It's important to keep in mind at this point that the actual design activities and outcomes will be different with every project and every team. However, there are some universal principles relevant to your team and to *you* as the leader of the entire 5D process.

YOUR ROLE AS THE LEADER IN THE DESIGN PHASE

First let's look at the role you might play in a traditional design project. You sit behind your desk. You describe to your team a general idea of a vague notion that's been on your mind. You say "-ish" a lot: "green-ish," "tall-ish," "formal-ish, but not too stuffy." Then you say those words that make even you cringe inside: "I can't explain exactly what I'm thinking, but I know I'll know it when I see it." Then you send your team off to their respective offices (or cubicles) to figure out (and maybe even fight over) what they think you just said.

You might even be thinking that you just delegated an important task; and maybe you're even feeling proud of yourself for "letting go" of control over something that's important to you. That's what great leaders do, right? But all you really did was to fragment your staff, ask them to read your mind, and maybe set up some of them for failure.

That's not what you want. You want a cohesive team, each holding the same ideas in their minds and working together to achieve that goal. So let's now look at your total experience design project and your role in it.

By now your entire project team (ideally your entire staff, even community members and customers) has gone through Discover, Dream, and

Define together. Because they have dreamed together, they hold in their hearts and minds the same shared picture of *their* organization's ideal future. What it will look like. What kinds of people *their* organization will serve. How everyone will feel serving those people and how *their* customers or clients will feel being served by *them*.

Notice that this is no longer *your* project. It's not even your organization, really, as it's undergoing this metamorphosis. You may have come to your team with the initial germ of an idea for a change. But since everyone has been through this process together (especially the Dream and Define phases), everyone has a stake in how the future organization will emerge from all their ideas. They own the outcome as much as you do. Because they will be sifting the various decisions through the same filters that they identified, as a team they will come to group conclusions as to which choices and investments will manifest their vision most closely to that which they have developed together.

So what could possibly be your role as a leader when you have just handed over the keys to the dream? Imagine yourself as the conductor of a world-class orchestra. You are supremely confident in each musician's ability to play their instrument at the expected level of proficiency. And you know that each section of the orchestra (strings, percussion, brass, woodwinds, etc.) is a well-practiced, unified entity in itself. What's your job as the conductor? To go to an oboe player and tell him precisely how to play his part of the symphony note for note? Perhaps reminding him that at the moment, the cellist is in line for the next pay raise? Or apologizing to the timpanist that she can't have new mallets because the reeds for the woodwinds have depleted the budget? Of course not.

As the conductor, your job is to unify all the departments of your organization. They are each focused on their own tasks (their parts) but must somehow come together, joining their individual contributions to the unified whole. This is where you come in.

Just as with a symphony conductor, your job is quite literally hands-off, trusting your talent to do their jobs well with support and guidance from you—not interference. You are working with the same master plan from which your orchestra is working (in the musicians' case, the music on the printed page; in your case, the vision and drivers). You leave the details up to your departments and their team leaders (in the orchestra's case that would be the concertmaster, who is also First Violin, the position which acts as a liaison between the conductor and the rest of the orchestra). You are there to make sure everyone has what they need to work in harmony, reading off the same page (both literally and figuratively speaking), and coordinating with each other to make sure the right tasks are completed in the right order and at the right time.

Your role is also to give your team the chance to create the best designs, even if it takes multiple attempts (see The Role of Iteration below). This may try your patience and frustrate your faith that your transformation will ever be accomplished. And that frustration may tempt you to give up the 5D process and jump in to interfere. Remember the conductor again: no orchestra plays an unfamiliar symphony flawlessly the first time. Orchestras get rehearsals. Your team gets iterations—multiple chances to improve on their ideas to arrive at the best possible variations on their vision.

THE ROLE OF YOUR EXPERIENCE DESIGN TEAM

Up until now your experience design team has worked together to create the dream of the future organization. As a group they identified their vision for the enterprise and the drivers that will help them manifest that vision. And then, again as a group, they identified the gaps that separate your dream enterprise from your current one. During this time, everyone has been working cross-functionally, even contributing ideas and inspirations to parts of the overall plan that may have little or nothing to do with their own individual departments or areas of expertise. Silos disappeared during this time, which is the best way to create conditions for fresh insights into otherwise unfamiliar functional areas.

But now that everyone is in the Design phase, the time has come for them to return to their silos and work on aspects of the vision that pertain specifically to their areas of expertise. The marketing people work on the marketing plan. The R&D people work on new product development. The building engineers work on determining whether the current layout of the floors and electrical systems will support the new vision. The people in HR work on identifying the talent you already have in place who will help bring your dream to reality, as well as designing new recruitment approaches to reach out to potential hires who will help build and sustain that dream.

No one is completely working in a vacuum, of course, because they have all heard from each other during the Dream and Define phases. Additionally, new relationships were developed during those phases, so it's now a simple matter of picking up the phone, walking down the hall, or sending a quick email to double-check an idea with the other team members. Still, the main focus of all the members of your team at this point is to find ways of closing those gaps they identified in the Define phase, and to design the ways in which their particular areas of expertise can close those gaps.

But their individual efforts and contributions must still be collected, organized, and managed to serve the big picture of your dream enterprise. Recall that in the orchestra analogy there is also the concertmaster—the person whose role is to serve as liaison between the musicians and the conductor (in other words, you). In this case your concertmaster is actually a group of people, making up a steering (or *core*) committee to help manage the flood of ideas and solutions that emerge from your team. Your core committee will be primarily responsible for organizing, integrating, and timing the designs and deciding which will actually be implemented for delivery. Ideally, the core committee should be made up of a diverse group of leaders from the various functions of your organization (or the 4Ps) and should also include high-potential visionaries you have identified as the ones most likely to carry the dream forward into the future. This group must be empowered by you to make decisions that allow the organizational transformation to move forward, on time, and on budget. Your job is to be clear about the authority they have, and don't have. In other words, they need to know from you when they can act, and when they need to bring you into the picture.

One by one, ideas for closing the gaps between your present organization and your future organization will emerge and be presented. Some will be immediately embraced and scheduled for implementation. Some will be immediately discarded, specifically because they run counter to the vision or values of your future entity—never because the originator of the idea is out of favor with the group or the leader.

To keep the creativity flowing freely, everyone should remember that there is no such thing as a bad idea. Each idea is the foundation or inspiration of a better one.

THE ROLE OF ITERATION

You should expect most ideas to go through various iterations before the final version is set in stone. If you (as the leader) are so goal oriented that iterations feel like a frustrating waste of time, you're not alone.

To some impatient leaders, iterations may feel like a series of false starts—consuming both time and precious resources. But in the end, repeated visits to the same solution have multiple benefits. They serve to not only improve that original idea or solution but also to prevent extremely costly mistakes from becoming permanent commitments to the final version of your dream organization. They also can help involve or bring along reluctant or skeptical participants, people who may not be able to believe in the big picture but who can at least commit to the interim steps.

"Iteration is not only how ideas are improved, it's how we come to understand the idea in the first place," says Leslie Marquard, managing director of Marble Leadership Partners, a Chicago-based corporate strategy and business transformation consultancy.

Most organizations typically invest in one or two iterations of an idea and then feel rushed to call it *done*. But when you bring together multiple models from a variety of perspectives—even from multiple opposing positions—that's where real innovation happens. Your team members hear or see an idea or point of view that they hadn't considered before. And the iteration process gives more people the chance to actually commit to the outcome—even if that outcome diverges from their own contributed ideas.

"When people have their hands in the process of creating the solution, they are much more wedded to making that solution a success than they would be if it was just presented to them as a *fait accompli*," says Marquard. "We shouldn't design things and then force them on people. We should design things that involve people. They become part of the process and they'll see that those things that they care about most will somehow become resident in the ultimate solution."

Iterations also show up in the form of mock-ups—three dimensional models of an idea or solution built to scale. Mock-ups have immense value in helping to prove a concept—to discover what works, what doesn't work, and to attract essential talent. For example, one midwestern hospital undergoing a complete revisioning of how it would present itself as a patient-centered health care provider to women needed a new medical director. The board identified a promising physician based in San Diego for that position. The challenge was to attract her away from San Diego and all its delights. The physician had her doubts but visited the center as a courtesy. She was an immediate convert to the dream when she saw the mock-up of the redesigned patient room. The innovative design for the room expressed the dream in a way that was unmistakably tangible, as well as exciting and enticing.

Likewise, in New Mexico, when the staff tried out a mock-up for the San Juan Regional Medical Center, they were impressed by the concept of single patient rooms featuring private screened porches, which provide additional family space as well as energy savings due to the deep shade they create. Still, some staff had doubts about the suggested fabric on the pull-out beds (proposed in each room for use by visiting friends and family members) until they had the opportunity to spill every kind of fluid imaginable in a hospital setting onto the upholstery and to watch how quickly and easily it cleaned up.

Through the mock-up process, they also discovered an important change that needed to be made to the patient bathrooms. As lovely as the bathrooms were, with their natural stone features, it was decided to make the rooms larger. The mock up demonstrated to the staff that should a patient fall in a bathroom, more room for two staff members to get in and help the patient would make for a safer experience. Changes made during the Design phase

Mock-up of a redesigned patient room. *Photo © Kahler Slater, Inc.*

The finished product—an actual patient room. *Photo by Steve Hall, Hedrich Blessing.*

due to the use of mock-ups avoided more costly changes later on, saving time and money.

Mock-ups have enduring utility beyond just the original "let's try it out and see if it works" purpose. At the Martha Jefferson Hospital, which is building a new hospital to replace its original downtown Charlottesville location, the administrators have kept the mock-up room open in the old hospital while the new hospital continues under construction outside of town. This way, staff can use the mock-up room for training and to get accustomed to new processes and procedures that will be in place when the new hospital opens.

As a leader you need tolerance for multiple attempts at a single outcome. And your team needs to be tolerant of multiple iterations as well. But paradoxically, you also need people on your team who do get impatient with many versions of solutions to a single problem. Otherwise, you risk analysis paralysis and nothing moving forward.

"You have to respect both working processes, plus all the ones which fall somewhere between the two extremes," says Marquard. "We need the big dream thinkers who never want to close the project down. But we cannot resist the contribution of the person who is a once-and-done kind of thinker, so that projects get completed."

Marquard points out that the iteration process also is extremely valuable in bringing along those who are resisting change altogether. Perhaps the resistance comes from the fact that they can't see the big picture for all the gaps that lie between the here and now and the ideal future. As Marquard says:

> You can use iterations like lily pads. Imagine crossing a pond by stepping on each lily pad and gaining confidence as each one holds you up. The iteration process is like that. For people who are resisting change because they can't see far enough ahead to have faith in the power of the final result, you can move them one lily pad at a time. You can take the whole group with you that way. All of a sudden you have carried someone who can't see past the end of his nose 15 years into the future. And he gets it. This is how alignment happens, one small change at a time—even if that change is only an imaginary one, on paper.

THE POWER OF PLAY IN BREAKTHROUGH DESIGN

It's been said that all work and no play makes Jack a dull boy. It also makes Jack not very inventive. Consider the Silicon Valley headquarters of some of the most innovative companies on the planet. As these entrepreneurs seek their first infusion of serious funding, it would seem to be a foregone conclusion that there is money in the budget for foosball tables, video games, a ping-pong table, maybe a half-pipe for skateboarding, a basketball court, certainly a fitness center, and even in some cases a swimming pool. To the casual observer, it would appear that maybe recruiters are bribing junior geniuses from the best colleges who are still distracted and lured in by the promise of fun. But there appears to be a method to their madness. These young masters of the technological universe may look like they're goofing off. But instead they are letting their subconscious have a whack at the challenges before them while they indulge in a pickup game with people from distant parts of their company's organization chart.

As it turns out, play is important for establishing a trusting and creative environment where people can lose themselves in developing breakthrough solutions to life's challenging problems. You don't need a half-pipe or even a ping-pong table to enjoy the same innovation advantages that the Silicon Valley masterminds employ every day. Boxes of crayons, tape, glue, paper clips, big sheets of paper, and the willingness to lose yourself into experimentation and fantasy is sometimes all you really need.

In his 2008 speech on the Power of Play before the annual Art Design Center Conference, Tim Brown (CEO of the innovation and design firm IDEO) said, "Playfulness helps us get to better solutions, helps us do our jobs better, and helps us feel better when we do them." He then outlined three different categories of play that help his own designers come up with design solutions as diverse as CD players, kidney transplant systems, immunization patches, supply chain design, new lobbies for the Marriott Courtyard brand, and the experience offered to people who donate blood to the American Red Cross.

Exploration Play

In this kind of play, the object of your game is to get as many ideas out of your head and on paper (or blackboard or whiteboard) as possible. Mind mapping is one of these exercises in which a problem is thrown out to the group and a facilitator is tasked with writing down suggested ideas on a board for everyone to see. The ideas are randomly placed on the space (not categorized by the facilitator into lines and rows) to keep the free-flowing brainstorming going. At Kahler Slater, "free beer" always appears in our mind mapping sessions, no matter what the topic is. Brown said in his speech that the idea behind exploration play is to "get out of the way of our own ideas."

Construction Play

According to Brown, the early prototype for the computer mouse was a roll-on deodorant bottle. It's remarkable what ideas can be generated from what Brown describes as "multiple low-resolution prototypes made from found items." In a sense, prototypes are physical metaphors for the ideal product. All you need is that box of crayons, tape, bits and pieces from everyday life, perhaps colorful modeling clay, and your imagination.

Role Play

This is essential in total experience design, because the emphasis is on the experience you are offering your stakeholders. One of the best ways to understand the experience of your customers is to put yourself in their shoes. Role playing might be the hardest play in which to indulge, especially if you or your design team are shy or introverted. But the value of pretend is that it reveals subtleties and nuances of an experience that you might not have discovered if only observing from afar. Experience Audits, such as the simulated knee surgery experience that Sharon and Jeff went through, are a form of role play, for instance.

In another example, when Kahler Slater experience designers were working on designing a new women's health center in the midwest, we role-played the entire hospital first impression experience in a borrowed hotel ballroom. We set up the room as we proposed it to be arranged to support their redesigned hospital greeting and registration process for women coming to the center for a wide variety of reasons, from delivering a baby to visiting inpatient family members; from office visits to physician specialists to education classes, health assessments, or screenings. We mocked up a foam core fireplace, water feature, café, and structural columns to define seating areas and travel paths, using banquet tables for the reception desk and borrowed hotel lobby furniture for seating. The experience started with the entry canopy and the valet staff who would greet visitors at their cars or at the door if they self-parked.

Hospital staff and the experience design team played the roles of patients and family interacting with the actual staff who would ultimately implement the intended redesigned experience. A wide variety of experiences were mocked up, such as an expectant couple arriving at 2:00 A.M., directly at the front door of the center rather than at the emergency room door (having a healthy baby at night is not an emergency, but many hospitals lock all doors except the emergency room door after visiting hours are over, say 8:00 P.M.). One of the nurses portrayed an elderly woman (in a wheelchair and pulling an oxygen tank on wheels) coming for a bone density scan to test for osteoporosis. Another designer played the role of a woman coming to the center for a simple mammogram screening. Each role player was preregistered and greeted at the door. Most needed nothing more than to go directly to their destination for care, which was confirmed the night before by phone, thus assuring no need to even stop at a front reception desk.

The entry lobby mock-up for the women's health center. *Photo © Kahler Slater, Inc.*

During the mock-up, a *cycle of service* was mapped out on newsprint pads, recording all touchpoints and documenting the desired patient or visitor experiences. The hospital's service coordinator staff took charge of this aspect of the process so they could follow through on developing staff service protocols, just as hotel managers do for their staff, and to support training and orienting of new staff.

One service expectation that was discovered was the need to let the staff in the ambulatory services areas know that the patient had arrived and to let the patient know if the staff were running on schedule. During the mock–up role play, the need to close this gap in service transition from reception to caregiver was identified and documented. The designed method to achieve this transition in the most personalized way was for the reception staff to send a message to other staff that their patient had arrived, using a system that already existed: the hospital's email system. The receptionist also added some personal descriptive information about the patient to the email message (color of clothing, for instance) so that when the staff would come into the patient lounge area, the staff member could walk right up to the patient and confirm his or her name, rather than swinging the door open and broadcasting the patient's name, thus maintaining a dignified and personal experience (which were identified in the visioning session as key Project Drivers).

During this role play, the women's health center designers discovered it was important that center reception staff understood the entire experience to make their portion of the experience seamless with the other experiences

The women's health center lobby redesign brought to life. *Photo by Steve Hall, Hedrich Blessing.*

provided by other staff. They also discovered that it was important for all staff to be able to answer questions about what happens next when asked by patients, even if they were talking with someone who wouldn't be a part of that experience. Instead of saying, "I don't know what happens next," the staff members would know and could thus help provide an ideal total experience rather than a fragmented series of less-than-ideal experiences. Once this new training program and orientation protocol were completed and implemented, the patient satisfaction scores for this area, which had been previously disappointing, were significantly improved, thus achieving the overall Project Vision.

Play is fun. No doubt about it. Play also loosens up the minds and imaginations of your team, forging new friendships, strengthening trust, sparking laughter, resulting in the thrill of breakthrough moments. Out of play will come amazing design solutions that will close the gaps you found in the Define phase and take your enterprise closer to its transformation.

CONCLUSION

If you're starting a brand new business from scratch, lucky you. You can build and create without having to change or demolish first. But if you're making radical changes to your current enterprise, you probably have a substantial list of gaps that need to be closed during your Design phase. And this is good. It means that you've established your bar of expectations high enough to really see significant and meaningful differences once your transformation is complete.

And this is where you start getting very specific with your choices moving forward. Do you have to make all the changes at once? That would be ideal, certainly. But sometimes it's unrealistic. For instance, you shouldn't fire your entire staff *en masse* just because you have decided one of your drivers is that your company will be warm and friendly to your customers (provided, of course, that your current batch of employees most decidedly aren't warm and friendly). But you can certainly install some training programs to help some of the more promising employees adjust to the changes.

Say that your team's new vision for the organization is that it projects a more upscale image in a safer neighborhood. You may not be able to move your business (lock, stock, and barrel) to another part of town. But maybe you can set up an interim budget to create signage and curb appeal that would make your place of business more enticing. At least by knowing what results you're aiming to achieve, you can make all the design choices and changes when they make sense to you, and when you have the time and resources to do so.

As long as you have the entire set of 4Ps addressed—even if only in your business plan for the next one to four quarters, or even further into the future—you will be working according to a plan specifically designed to ultimately manifest your authentic transformation.

Chapter 9

DELIVER—THE FINISH AND THE STARTING LINE

Changes are not only possible and predictable, but to deny them is to be an accomplice to one's own unnecessary vegetation.

Gail Sheehy

Photo by Comstock/Media Bakery.

DELIVER

Time is money, of course. And any fiscally accountable leader would naturally ask, "How long does a process like this take to deliver an authentic total experience design transformation?" And, equally naturally, the answer could only be: it depends. Variables include the complexity of your transformation, size of the project, the number of teams involved in the decision-making process, how committed the senior-most leaders are to being full participants from the very beginning. But one thing is certain: The 5D process helps you identify all the major drivers and gaps at the very beginning, which will ultimately save you valuable time (and potentially costly missteps) as you go deeper into the process. The investment in the time you spend upfront will be more than returned by the time you save as you go.

Authentically Google in Madison, Wisconsin—an open, collaborative, and fun office experience. *Photo by Al Gartzke, Milwaukee.*

When Google decided to open a new office in Madison, Wisconsin, the leadership knew what they wanted from the start. Because of that certainty, which was articulated and confirmed during a quick, three-hour Visioning Workshop (and because they are Google, where everything seems to move at warp speed), the new office experience was designed and up and running in a record five months from start to finish. What did they want? A location that was downtown, on the east side of Madison—the bohemian, creative, artsy center of creativity and innovation, which is what Google is all about. Google also wanted a location that provided an alternative to a car-based commuting culture, so it had to be easily accessible by public transportation and bike paths, attesting to their environmental awareness, as well as the kind of talent they recruit who share this same commitment. It wanted the new location to incorporate the key aspects of authentic Google corporate culture: an open, innovative and collaborative environment that is a fun place to be.

And, as is the case with its offices throughout the world, Google wanted its new office design to reference the community in which it is located. It wanted this office to be clearly a Google office—but the *Madison, Wisconsin,* office—not just an extension of the main campus in Mountainview, California.

What would be "Wisconsin enough" to be undeniably Wisconsin? A number of ideas were generated—perhaps a nautical reference to the beautiful nearby lakes? Maybe. Or a thumbs up to the nearby and highly regarded University of Wisconsin–Madison, which serves as their primary source for recruits? The answer came clear and certain in the physical location for their Madison office—the International Harvester Building, an older, downtown industrial building that hadn't been renovated beyond recognition. Wisconsin's agricultural traditions! That's it!

The building itself had to undergo a design and technological update in order to be functional in its new purpose, and in keeping with their commitment to sustainability, Google retained as much of the building's materials and character as it could—using the big, original windows as interior conference room walls to promote that desired feeling of open collaboration. But when privacy is needed, staffers simply slide into place what used to be the doors of the freight elevators. The wavy, two-tone carpet is a reference to the juxtaposition between land and lake.

Just as Google is whimsical corporate-wide, two features in the lobby translate that whimsy into the uniquely agricultural vernacular. An actual International Harvester tractor cab has made its way back to the building and now serves as a phone booth. And, in keeping with the fun that Google famously has with its logo, the Google lobby sign is made up of antique farm implements assembled by a local artist. And, of course, whimsy isn't true whimsy unless it's over the top. So that sign is strung with lights that either

The whimsical Google Madison office lobby sign. *Photo by Al Gartzke, Milwaukee.*

shine Google's corporate colors or whichever colors represent the holidays— very much like what the Empire State Building does during holidays and festive occasions in New York City.

Google's site managers were able to deliver all of this in record time because they knew going in what their vision and Project Drivers were, based on the strong, well-defined, and authentic culture that is Google.

No project, no matter how well designed, means anything if it can't be appropriately delivered. Which means that all of the details of delivery must be attended to—schedules and budgets met, goals achieved, outcomes delivered. In a typical architectural design project, a *program manager* is often the one point person whose sole job it is to make sure these things happen. However, when you (as the leader) are asking your entire organization to transform itself in the service of authenticity and total experience design, *you* become the champion for this project. It's your job to ensure that the story is told authentically. You are the program manager, and it's up to you to shepherd the final D of the 5D process—Deliver.

As the leader, your responsibility is to ensure that your shared vision is carried out in every detail of every concept. So far, you have had plenty of help. Through the first four Ds, your team has helped you move through the process of Discover, Dream, Define, and Design. They have worked outside of their functional silos and within them to identify strategies that will close the gaps they discovered between your current status and your ideal organizational future in Define. And now that the group has discerned which strategies to implement and in what order, they are ready to get started delivering on those strategies. They're looking to you to help marshal that transformation from the old version of your organization to the new iteration of what kind of organization you as a group aspire to become.

Organizational change may not be easy, but it does follow a fairly predictable pattern. According to group dynamics theory as developed by Bruce Tuckman in the 1960s, all groups go through the following stages of development over time:

Forming

When groups are initially organized, a number of needs and questions arise. Members find their respective places and roles within the newly constituting group. They experience both the excitement of high expectations, as well as anxiety about how the organization will eventually take shape.

Storming

This stage is marked with frustration, impatience, disappointment, and confusion. Without strong leadership (and, at times, even with it) group members rebel against each other and often against authority. Goals, tasks, and action plans are unfamiliar as the group moves toward the transformed version of itself. And the insecurity in this phase charges the corporate culture with uncertainty and stress.

Norming

A track record of early successes begins to build harmony, trust, support, and respect among the team members. The increased confidence dissipates some of the tension and whatever internal turf struggles there might be. Group members are more open and willing to give feedback.

Performing

This stage describes the group at its most productive. The team members are working collaboratively and interdependently. They're confident in their new roles; they understand how the leader's role might have changed in the context of the new version of the enterprise. This is where there is truly a sense of great accomplishment among the team members.

All organizations follow this same pattern of development. However, in terms of group dynamics, whenever a team or organization experiences a significant change, such as when a new team member is added, or an organization suffers some great loss, disaster, or rapid growth, the dynamics start all over again. Knowing that this is a predictable pattern, teams can take heart in knowing that whatever upheaval they're experiencing is normal, natural, and won't last forever.[1]

An argument can be made for a fifth stage—*re-forming,* in which organizations must respond to marketplace changes and demands for new ideas and services. The people may remain the same, but the entire organization must be transformed to remain relevant in a changing world. Hardly any organization is immune to this stage, which can be a perfect invitation to a total experience redesign. On the other side of the same transformation coin, a total experience redesign is a perfect catalyst for reforming.

So, whether re-forming is the catalyst or the consequence of a total experience design in your enterprise, it will be up to you to deliver the leadership your team will require to help it process through all the changes smoothly. As you enter the Deliver phase of the 5Ds, you are asking your people to deliver an entirely new set of experiences to your stakeholders. Likewise, they need you to deliver to them the support, guidance, and reinforcement necessary to help them manifest the vision that you and your team have nurtured in its abstract for so long. Now it's time to really get real. Assuming, of course, you haven't done so already—which leads us to your own behaviors first.

AUTHENTIC CHANGE MUST START WITH YOU

Unless you're a brand new CEO of an already existing enterprise (in which case, as we've already discussed, it is probably too soon to lead this change initiative), much of what the enterprise is is a reflection of your own values and behaviors up until this point. So if what you desire is a changed organization retooled to deliver an authentic total experience design, don't wait until you're confident that the organizational change has permanently clicked into place before changing your own behaviors. You have to model the new way long before the rest of the organization is even aware that change is on the horizon.

What does that mean in practical terms? Be to all your employees how you expect them to be to each other, your customers, and your community. If you authentically value extraordinarily high levels of customer service enabled by employees empowered to make decisions on the spot, deliver extraordinarily high levels of service to your people. Not just your direct reports, but throughout the organization. Know people's names; be seen in the company cafeteria having real conversations with people—not just making the meet-and-greet rounds like a busy bride at a crowded reception. Be yourself, the relaxed and friendly version of you. Behave in the same, respectful way to your entire staff as you would to your partners or board of directors.

Be sure you're seen at all events that the organization launches to manifest its new and better version of itself. If you want the people in your organization to build healthy lifestyle habits, be seen at the salad bar, out on the walking paths around your facility, on the basketball court, at the gym. If you want your organization to take the lead in community social responsibility, be seen swinging a hammer at a Habitat for Humanity project (really swinging that hammer for the full day, not just making a few desultory taps for the camera while wearing spotless chinos and a polo shirt).

If you want to encourage your organization to take more creative risks at problem solving or opening new markets, take risks yourself. You don't have to be Richard Branson, piloting high-tech balloons around the planet. And you don't have to invest in space tourism. There are plenty of business boundaries you can test with both feet on the ground—succeeding wildly at some, failing at others. Whatever the outcome, be sure your people know it and observe the way you manage both successes and failures.

Mahatma Gandhi said, "You must be the change you wish to see in the world." You personally should be modeling and even delivering authentic and positive total experiences internally long before your people have a clue that a change is in store for them as well.

INSTALL AN ACCOUNTABILITY CULTURE, NOT A BLAMING ONE

As your people start understanding that change is in their future, they're going to want to know exactly how that will influence the way they work and serve your stakeholders. Of course, they'll soon find out that they themselves will be part of the Dreaming team to identify what those changed behaviors will be. When they've identified those changed behaviors, that's when they will be accountable for helping to see the changes through.

But making this transformation won't be as simple (or as instantaneous) as flipping a switch. Even if they sincerely want to, people don't change that quickly, especially if they have been historically rewarded for behaving in different ways. There will be slip-ups—even from you.

Make those incidences teachable moments instead of blaming situations in which someone is punished or set up as an example. When you make a mistake, be the first to say so and open a discussion around what everyone can learn from the experience.

This is actually an essential part of an accountability culture. A culture that emphasizes accountability is not necessarily a punishing, blaming, or stifling one. A culture that celebrates accountability is one in which people can trust each other to keep their promises. This kind of trust frees them to focus on *their* work and deliverables, fully expecting that the people they are counting on will come through.

When it comes to launching a major transformation initiative (especially one that is as integrated as total experience design), everyone must fully understand how their efforts dovetail with everyone else's. So, while slip-ups can be expected and forgiven, nothing is more demoralizing to sincerely motivated high performers than a pattern of nonperformers repeatedly being given a pass on broken promises or failed objectives.

MAKE SURE YOUR GOALS AND OBJECTIVES ALIGN WITH YOUR PRIORITIES

Just as your staff won't be transforming overnight with the flip of a switch, your business will be transforming gradually as well. If you're just starting the transformation process, you may be firmly positioned on the far left of the continuum between the Old Organization and the New Organization. That's a natural place for you to be right now. And your projects and processes may be firmly ensconced in that place as well.

Does this mean you turn down all initiatives that have kept you busy in your years as the Old Organization? You're the leader, so it's up to you—depending on your organization's priorities as a transforming enterprise. Unless you are radically changing your values, you will find that it's reasonable to gradually change the mix of Old to New Organization projects to most closely match the manifestation of your group's new dream.

In the meantime, certainly one of your priorities as a leader is to keep your organization a vibrant, viable one that keeps itself financially sustained and its employees, well, employed through the process. You still have priorities as a leader that keep you tied (however temporarily) to the Old Organization.

Don't automatically turn away all work that comes your way because you're still known by your stakeholders in terms of your Old Organization version. Just be aware of what types of projects slow down your transformation and what types actually help you and your stakeholders along that path to change. Slowly phase out the projects and opportunities that keep you tied to the past in order to make room for New Organization opportunities.

GET PEOPLE UP-TO-SPEED QUICKLY

If you take advantage of the 5D process, you will have incorporated many, if not all, of your stakeholders or their representatives in planning the transformation. So these essential changes should not come as a huge surprise to most people with whom you engage on a regular basis. Still, there will be some who just refuse to get it, at least the first few times you remind them that your organization is undergoing a significant metamorphosis. It's also only fair that you be patient with those who weren't included in the 5D process. Perhaps you are being contacted by a new potential client who comes to you via a referral from an old client, one who "didn't get the memo." The new client is coming to you because you are great at doing the Old Organization work—that's the reputation you have out there in the marketplace. It's going to take some time to move that reputation more toward the New Organization end of the continuum.

Move Your Internal Stakeholders toward Your New Organization

Hopefully, you'll experience little to no resistance—especially if you have included everyone in the transformation process. Still, you might have a few employees who were absolutely hitting their sweet spot in the Old Organization setting, and might feel threatened or challenged by change when they think about the New Organization way. Know who these people are. And treat them well because they are your key to sustaining your success as you and your other employees move your organization toward the future. They are actually an asset at this point because they are freeing up your other talent to move toward your dream. They are there to take care of your long-standing customers and stakeholders who still expect the same menu, the same products and services. They can ultimately be the New Organization's ambassadors to these long-standing clients, many of whom you also may want to retain as you make your organizational changes.

You can still take these Old Organization employees with you as the New Organization takes on a life and viability of its own. They have had the chance to observe how your changes are unfolding and watch as your New Organization's track record of successes mount up and you invest more and more of your resources in that end of the continuum. While some may decide that the changes don't match their own ambitions or values and decide to move on, you'll find that many of the people whom you want to keep will enthusiastically embrace the transformed organization and their roles in it. They just may have needed a little bit of extra help and time to catch up with their colleagues who were already onboard.

The most painful separations, of course, will be to those employees whom you cherish and respect for their contributions through the years but who don't fit into the transformed culture no matter how hard they try to make the fit. Those separation decisions will be difficult and heartbreaking, to be sure. But as your organization continues to move in the direction of full transformation, the day may come when you will be forced to have painful discussions with some excellent and valued people. Hopefully, as painful as those conversations may be, they won't come as a terrible shock and surprise. Everyone should have the equal chance to move into the future along with the organization. Those who don't, won't, because they will have chosen not to or because they become fully aware that their skill sets or passions no longer fit with the organization's new direction.

Move Your External Stakeholders toward Your New Organization

Depending on the nature of your enterprise, your external stakeholders could be your customers, members, clients, or patients; citizens of your local community or market; taxpayers; even competitors and/or practitioners of associated businesses or services. Ideally you included key representatives of these groups in your Discover, Dream, Define, and Design phases, so they have already been recruited as your partners in transformation.

But not everyone will be paying attention. So you have to keep reminding them that you are no longer who you once were. Frequent communication, press releases, letters, invitations to celebrations marking the transformation, new taglines designed to describe your new self in a quick sound bite, and a new logo might help. You will have to keep repeating your new message and reminders. It will eventually sink in with some. With others, it never will.

Continue to service those resistant external stakeholders for as long it makes sense for you to do so (and as long as you have the appropriate talent necessary to do it well). But don't hang on to those relationships when they start holding you back from making the total transformation that you have identified as your New Organization. Eventually you will phase out these relationships—perhaps referring them to your former employees who would be a better match for their needs.

Go where no one knows you. Launching a marketing initiative from Square One may seem like an exhausting proposition. But it's also exhausting having to constantly remind people that you are no longer who you once were. Don't abandon your loyal external stakeholders entirely, of course. But use your transformation as a valuable opportunity to open new markets. If you're local, go regional. If you're regional, expand to other regions—maybe even go national. If you're national, go international. Every major change can be a crisis. Intentional changes are good crises. Why waste a good crisis?

DELIVER YOUR FUTURE NOW

Just as having a Tangible Image of the future is a critical part of any Organizational Vision Statement, so, too, is it vitally important to paint as complete a picture of the New Organization as possible for those whom you want and need to help you realize that future. One way to do so is to ask your employees and their teams to write their page in your organization's annual report of the future. At Kahler Slater, we asked all business and operational teams to imagine a time 15 years into the future, and to compose a page in the organization's annual report describing what this future will be like. What kinds of clients would they be serving? What products and services would they be offering? Where and how would they be doing their work? What kind of experts would they have become? What kinds of awards or accolades would they have received?

While these annual reports were fantasy, they also informed us in deep detail what our evolution could be in the future. They were exciting and inspiring, to be sure, and they also helped us recruit new talent. As candidates came closer to being offered a position, we would hand them these annual reports and ask them to read them. Then we would say, "Do you see yourself helping us to get here in the next 15 years? If so, what specifically would you do to help us achieve these goals?"

CELEBRATE YOUR TEAM'S ACCOMPLISHMENTS

As you lead your organization through the 5Ds and the transformation that will put it on the path to a new authenticity, realize that all your stakeholders are pioneers in this effort, especially your employees. They are putting their careers on the line for the sake of this change. Even the ones who are wholeheartedly aligned with your shared vision are turning their backs on the familiar to reach for the unknown. They deserve to know when they've achieved specific goals. And they should be celebrated for those accomplishments. They also should be celebrated for taking risks—even if those risks fail in some way.

They are your employees, and as such their job is to deliver new, total experiences to your customers and other stakeholders. You are their leader. Your job is to deliver your enthusiasm, support and encouragement at every opportunity. Don't wait for the entire transformation journey to be completed before you give them the kudos they deserve. Those interim milestone celebrations will keep them focused and encouraged.

MEASURE YOUR RESULTS

In architecture and interior design, there is the convention of post-occupancy evaluations (POEs). This measurement process or tool evaluates whether or not the design goals of the project were achieved. The evaluation can be accomplished through surveys, observations, interviews and/or through focus groups.

For example, a post-occupancy evaluation for the Marquette University School of Dentistry included interviewing students, patients, faculty, and staff, and it was implemented seven years after the school launched the new curriculum in a new facility. The evaluation assessed whether or not the Project Vision and Project Drivers (established at the start of the project) were realized. Those interviewed at Marquette several years after the transformation was complete—some of whom were also part of the original planning and design process—confirmed the importance of consensus building as they took ownership of the choices that they made during visioning, and continue to do so now.

Associative outcomes uncovered during data collection for the Marquette post-occupancy evaluation show that since the building's opening, the school has enjoyed a doubling of the number of student applications with a yield rate (applicants who accept the university's offer to learn at their school) in the 70th percentile—equivalent to the likes of Harvard undergrad yield rates. Additionally, patient, student, and faculty satisfaction scores typically rate at the top of the scale (90 to 95 percent), or in the "good to very good" category, with questions related to areas such as "facility comfort/pleasantness," "level of technology," and "likelihood of recommending the school to others." School administration and staff interviewed also reported that the new experience and environment are key elements in attracting and retaining top faculty and students.

Every industry has different methods of measuring the success of its activities. Whatever approach you use, an essential aspect of Deliver is ascertaining that you're delivering what you promised and determining whether your stakeholders are satisfied. If the answer is yes, then find out specifically what makes them satisfied. If the answer is no, find out specifically what the disconnect is and why. You don't know if you're successfully fulfilling the Deliver phase of the 5Ds until you find out exactly how well you're doing.

For internal stakeholders, employee engagement surveys measure their likelihood of staying and delivering above-and-beyond quality of work to your organization. You also can find out which managers and supervisors are particularly gifted in employee engagement, and which ones are putting your culture at risk for behaviors that run counter to your New Organization promise.

As for your external stakeholders, satisfaction surveys designed specifically to the nature of your enterprise will tell you where you need to improve. If you're losing an extraordinary number of stakeholders (if people are quitting at an unusual rate or if you're losing customers), surveys may tell you why and how to fix it.

However you approach your measurements, make sure the results you gather are both quantifiable and qualifiable. Be sure you can understand the stories and reasons why behind the numbers.

How Do You Know that You've Arrived?

You have arrived when the culture, norms, vision and mission of your New Organization have taken hold internally. Everyone throughout your entire organization is fluent in the new way. People can speak in terms of your organization's values, and how staff behave according to those values, day in and day out. They have stories to tell about how your employees lived out those values—even in the face of temptation to revert to told ways.

Your longtime stakeholders can't remember a time when it hasn't been *this way.* In fact, your New Organization is no longer New. It just is.

When you ask the abundance of new applicants why they want to work for your company, their answers unmistakably align with your vision and purpose. They're motivated specifically by the very characteristics that you and your team designed to launch your transformation.

In meetings, you find that your staff finishes your and each other's sentences. They care about the same things you care about and you're pulling together as a unified team in the New Organization way. You're more profitable than you have ever been, doing the kind of work you've always dreamed of doing. You might still have Old Organization stakeholders (either employees or customers), but everyone welcomes and is excited about the trend in the direction of the New Organization.

Finally, you send customers and potential employees in the direction of your former competitors. You are happy to share. Why? Because you are so authentically different, you cease to have competition.

You've made it real. But don't think you're finished. While your vision will remain constant, external forces, fashion, and financial considerations will always exert pressure on your enterprise to evolve and grow.

And the time will come to begin again.

EPILOGUE:
MAKE IT REAL

It's time for a business evolution that sets us on the path leading toward organizations striving to offer their best and most authentic selves to a public hungry for it. This desire for authenticity is being played out in the return of boutique and specialty retail to communities large and small. The days of the corner bakery or mom-and-pop diner are back after a glut of chain store, more-of-the-same product offerings. Not that there's anything wrong with the chain store product and service delivery model—Gap, Inc., for instance, has made it easy for me to get stylish jeans at the right price. And all I have to do is visit the mall closest to my house to make it happen, confident that the item I want will be in stock. It's easy. Gap is everywhere, and because I know that one Gap is pretty much like all the rest, this provides me with a sense of confidence and ease in my life. And who wouldn't be for increased confidence and ease (even if it's about buying sportswear)?

But lately, something different has replaced my need for confidence and ease. I want to eat really good bread, like the kind I tasted in France a few years ago. And I want to buy it from the guy who baked it, and who knows my name. I want to enter his corner shop, the one with the cute red-and-white striped awning, and take the chocolate chip cookie sample he offers me, still warm from the oven. I want to breathe in the aroma of fresh bread, and recall the simplicity of my own childhood along with the scent. I want to know for certain that I'm buying fresh bread made with natural ingredients that will nourish my family. I'll go out of my way to get to this shop, and pay more for the rye loaf than what I would pay at the big box supermarket down the street, because this 15-minute experience, including the "good to see you, Jill," and "goodbye, come again," which I get when I leave is worth it. Why? Because it makes me feel connected to the person who made the bread and to the community in which I live and in which this bakery exists. It's more than bread that I have purchased—it's an experience in which I've engaged, one human being connecting with another. It works because it's an exchange that is based on trust. It works because it's real. There's nothing fake about it.

That experience, for many in the world of small, boutique retail, is one which is fueled by the passion of the owner of the business. The baker who lives to feel flour up to his elbows, and who knows the value of saying hello and goodbye to each and every customer without being told by a consultant that it's good business to do so. The baker who designs and controls every aspect of the experience, from the staff he hires to serve me, to the way in which the shop is designed and the products are marketed, to the kind of bread that he offers on a daily basis. All of these decisions are his, and all are decided using his vision for the business as the primary filter for how he does business. The passion he feels for his bakery is evident in everything he does. His customers know it, see it, feel it, and experience it. It's as real as the bread coming out of his oven.

The challenge for all organizations and businesses today, small or large, boutique or chain, is to be like the baker—to find the passion in what you do, to create an authentic vision for it, and to infuse it into every facet of your organization. This isn't easy when your company might involve 10,000 people working in 32 different states. But since when did *easy* become a synonym for *great* or *successful?* Creating total experiences for all of your stakeholders based upon your organization's authentic vision, which results in a truly differentiating position in the marketplace, is really hard work. And it doesn't happen overnight. It takes time. Along the way, there will be challenges. You may mess up, a lot, in trying to find your way to your most authentic organizational self. But being real isn't about being perfect or flawless. In fact, your stakeholders (none of whom are perfect in their own right) will likely stick by you when you fall if they see you getting up again, to keep the promises that you made to them, and which brought them to you in the first place.

I believe that Margery Williams, author of the children's classic, *The Velveteen Rabbit or How Toys Become Real*, knew this when she wrote:

> "What is REAL?" asked the Rabbit one day, when they were lying side by side near the nursery fender, before Nana came to tidy the room. "Does it mean having things that buzz inside you and a stick-out handle?"
>
> "Real isn't how you are made," said the Skin Horse. "It's a thing that happens to you. When a child loves you for a long, long time, not just to play with, but REALLY loves you, then you become Real."
>
> "Does it hurt?" asked the Rabbit.

"Sometimes," said the Skin Horse, for he was always truthful. "When you are Real you don't mind being hurt."

"Does it happen all at once, like being wound up," he asked, "or bit by bit?"

"It doesn't happen all at once," said the Skin Horse. "You become. It takes a long time. That's why it doesn't happen often to people who break easily, or have sharp edges, or who have to be carefully kept. Generally, by the time you are Real, most of your hair has been loved off, and your eyes drop out and you get loose in the joints and very shabby. But these things don't matter at all, because once you are Real you can't be ugly, except to people who don't understand."[1]

THE KAHLER SLATER STORY

Designers are teaching CEOs and managers how to innovate. . . . They pitch themselves to businesses as a resource to help with a broad array of issues that affect strategy and organization—creating new brands, creating customer experiences, understanding user needs, changing business practices.

Bruce Nussbaum

So what does a relatively small design shop, which is more than a century old, headquartered in the midwest, know about authenticity and differentiation? Plenty. The architectural profession has seen rapid changes in the past 15 years unlike anything experienced in the previous 50. For us at Kahler Slater, the idea of practicing our craft in a new way that responds to the constantly evolving society in which we live, work, play, and learn was a business necessity that we needed to commit to if we planned to thrive for another 100 years. Additionally, the desire to do meaningful work in a way that positively transforms the businesses, organizations, and, indeed, the very lives of our clients and their customers, became our calling.

This was the basis for our own marketplace differentiation. So we had some work to do on ourselves. Our goal: to transform ourselves from a traditional architecture firm to an interdisciplinary enterprise that helps clients design total experiences for their customers and employees. Several catalysts during the decade beginning in the early 1990s helped to accelerate our transformation—the impending retirement of the firm's two leaders, David Kahler and Mac Slater, and the move to a new headquarters. These events provided an opportunity to rethink the entire organization, allowing us to respond to a rapidly changing world in new and better ways.

We first had to ask ourselves some fundamental questions. Who were we at our core? What did we want to represent to our clients during our own transformation from a traditional architecture firm to an interdisciplinary enterprise that designs total experiences? And with what kinds of clients did we want to work? Answer: altruistic leaders who have a vision of the extraordinary possibilities that emerge from the opportunity to transform themselves.

Visionary clients are not content with the status quo, with doing business as usual. They see a better way, a better outcome, and often they need assistance in articulating and implementing their vision. It's not about *our* vision. It's about the vision our clients have for themselves; for their organizations, employees, and vendors; and for their customers.

In our work, visionary leaders are calling into question who they are, in an organizational capacity, and who they wish to become. Change the outward manifestation of an organization—its physical environment—and the opportunity to challenge and/or change everything else becomes readily apparent. The opportunity of a new building offers visionary leaders a golden chance to rethink who they are, how they wish to be perceived, what products and services best reflect how they serve their customers, whom they hire, and how they operate. Having a clear vision for the future of the organization serves as the primary or essential filter for taking apart the organization and putting it back together again.

We provide a process and, more importantly, an attitude that supports, encourages, and focuses on defining the vision for the experiences desired by our clients. Working with them in the design of *total experiences,* rather than only the design of bricks and mortar, has propelled our firm from a leading regional provider of architecture and interior design services to an interdisciplinary design firm working with clients all over the world. But getting there has taken some purposeful and transformational experiences of our own.

A BRIEF HISTORY OF KAHLER SLATER

Fitzhugh Scott founded the firm in 1908. Fitz, as he was known, was an up-and-coming architect in Milwaukee, with a circle of influential and wealthy friends who often called upon him for design services. But not all of his acquaintances were wealthy. In 1915, two friends approached him and invited him to design a manufacturing plant for a new electrical switch they had just invented. The only catch was that Fitz would have to postpone any fees from the commission, as the inventors didn't have any money to pay him for his services. Confident that the inventors would achieve success, Fitz designed the plant, including its famous clock tower (its four faces making it the largest four-sided clock in the world, larger even than London's Big Ben) for what would become Allen-Bradley, and later, Rockwell Automation. Throughout the years, the firm added other high profile clients and projects, including the master plan and some of the early buildings for Vail, Colorado, and numerous projects for campuses in the growing University of Wisconsin system.

In 1965, Fitzhugh Scott, Jr., who was then the head of the firm that his father founded, tapped David Kahler, an assistant professor of architecture at the University of Illinois, to take over the leadership of the firm. And, in turn, Kahler invited Mac Slater to be his partner, transforming the firm into Kahler Slater.

During the recession of 1992, while many Wisconsin architecture firms were forced to reduce staff, Kahler Slater actually added employees as our client list grew. While our design expertise and excellent reputation kept clients knocking at our door, market research with our past and current clients confirmed that our ability to provide excellent service is what kept clients coming back. It also prompted them to recommend our firm to others. So it was something about the *experience* of working with us, in addition to the outcome of a well-designed environment, that was spurring our growth. Recognizing this, we embarked on a year-long exploration of our design and service experience. So 1995 was dubbed, "The Year of the Client," and it kicked off with our firm forming internal work groups to discover what it was about our clients' experiences in working with us that we could strengthen and leverage throughout the organization.

PASSION PAVES THE WAY

We discovered that clients wanted to work with us because of our people, who were universally described as *passionate professionals*. What became obvious to us was that this passion served as both the basis and the source for future outstanding work. We realized that when our employees are doing work they are passionate about, our clients benefit because they get to work with highly motivated and enthusiastic people. The staff benefits because they work on projects that excite them. The result? Outstanding, award-winning projects. The firm itself prospers because the recognition and resulting repeat business allow us to do more work—and reinvest in our people.

We leveraged this insight by asking all our staff what they were passionate about, personally as well as professionally. We spent nearly the full year engaging our staff in a series of exercises and discussions designed to articulate and document a common vision for the organization. The resulting DNA of our own Vision Statement is something we believe would resonate with our founder, Fitzhugh Scott. Our Drivers of Progress, which we update regularly to reflect the new challenges and opportunities of a changing world, help us to refocus our efforts and continue to differentiate our company in an increasingly competitive marketplace.

Our Core Beliefs and Values are used as a filter for all of our hiring decisions. For instance, a fabulous designer who can't abide by our Core Belief and Value of respectful collaboration won't receive an employment offer from us, no matter how brilliant his or her portfolio of work may be.

These tenets also form the basis of our semiannual performance review and goal-setting process with all staff. If someone isn't sharing information or isn't accepting of new ideas, chances are that his or her review will include a discussion on our Core Belief and Value of openness.

As another example of how we use our vision as a filter for running our business, when we expressed our desire in our Mission Statement to "travel the globe to do our work," it was a signal to our IT staff. Lacking sufficient technological tools to enable our firm to work internationally at the time, we needed to focus some attention and resources toward achieving this goal. Having acquired the needed technological resources and operational skills,

Kahler Slater | VISION
experience design

DNA		DRIVERS OF PROGRESS	
Core Values WE BELIEVE DEEPLY IN:	**Purpose** WE EXIST TO:	**Mission** BY 12/2010 WE WILL:	**Tangible Image** WE ARE:
Relationships/Trust Respectful Collaboration Passion/Creativity Integrity Openness	Enhance life through artful design.	Partner with visionary and altruistic clients throughout the world. Design and manage innovative and transformational, life enhancing experiences for our clients, our clients' clients, and ourselves. Lead the full integration of Perception, People, Products/Services and Place with all of our clients. Secure and nurture the best people.	A trusted, leading enterprise sought after by people inspired to work with us in long-term relationships, in a positive, creative and collaborative atmosphere. Leading multi-sensory and interdisciplinary design processes that result in enhanced and sustainable performance for our clients. An interdisciplinary team of passionate, creative, diverse and technologically advanced experts willing to travel the globe to do their work. A growing, continuously innovating enterprise with expanding ownership and increasing profit.

Copyright © 2010 Kahler Slater, Inc.

we've begun our venture into foreign markets, with projects in Europe, the Middle East, and Asia. We opened our sixth office in June 2009 in Singapore.

Our mission of partnering with visionary and altruistic clients provides an additional filter that is enormously helpful in terms of our new business development efforts. We focus on finding and working with clients who fit the visionary (or the potential to be visionary) mold. We take great pride in working closely not only with visionary clients, but also with those who have a vision of doing well by doing good—leaders in noble and humanitarian causes, wherever they may be. And in the last few years, we've begun to work with clients who truly want to break the mold by bringing completely new ideas and services to the market, and need not only a new building to do so, but also an identity—a new name, brand, Web site, and other marketing materials—as well as an operational plan, hiring strategy, product packaging, and so forth. In other words, they need help designing the entire total experience of their new offering.

As we identified *visionary and altruistic clients* as our target market, we also were discovering through fresh perspectives exactly who we wanted to be internally, and what kinds of projects we wanted to take on. When we went through our own internal discovery sessions, we learned that Kahler Slater employees shared mutual passions for particular types of environments they loved to design. As a result, we formed design teams to serve specific markets. One team was assembled to become experts in environmentally sustainable architecture. Another team was built around health care because of a passion that had been ignited by negative personal health care experiences and the desire to create truly healing environments and patient-centered experiences. Our staff who were most interested in the world of academia formed a higher education team, dedicated to helping clients create collegiate environments and experiences to help students learn better, both in and out of the classroom, and to help faculty teach more effectively and creatively.

The entire Kahler Slater staff was included in these sessions—not just our design talent. Administrative staff, for instance, found renewed enthusiasm in taking to heart the firm's Purpose to "enhance life through artful design" and invested everything they did with their own artfulness and passion.

When we asked our staff, "What drives your passion?" the answers we received were the truth—but the truth didn't always make us happy. Several cherished and valued staffers decided that their passions were all about running their own small businesses. As sorry as we were to see them go, we also knew we had to support the pursuit of their passions—even if they weren't going to be Kahler Slater employees anymore. And so we offered them office space, business counsel, and even leads for potential projects and assignments. Kahler Slater has helped create quite a few new businesses through the years—architecture, interior design, graphic design, project management, and consulting firms—which have added to the richness of the communities in which we're located. From time to time, we have partnered with these former staff members in their new businesses. Our clients benefit, their clients benefit, and both businesses benefit from our mutual commitments to stay close with each other.

Kahler Slater also has grown in surprising directions in response to the passions that drive our employees. Some staffers have expressed their passion to deliver different kinds of services—beyond bricks and mortar—that they believed were wanted by clients, and are critical to the design of successful, total customer and employee experiences. These included facilitation and strategic planning services to help clients define and/or refine their vision and strategies for their projects and organizations. They also included marketing and graphic design services to help clients communicate and celebrate their newly integrated vision, plans and projects.

Consequently, we launched a consulting division. This began to differentiate our organization from those that simply designed buildings. It was at this point that we expanded our focus from designing *environments* to designing *experiences* to match those environments. We began looking at ourselves and our work from a new perspective. And we set out to transform our organization in a way that would allow us to do our best work, with a process and outcomes that would differentiate us in the marketplace.

At that time, the mid-1990s, we were a 65-person organization with one CEO and seven principal owners with a vision of a growing enterprise with expanded ownership and increasing profits. Since then, our DNA and Drivers of Progress have guided us to become a firm of 150 staff in six offices. We have three executive officers (3EOs) who share the office and responsibilities of CEO, and 48 owners—24 principals and 24 associate principals.

In 1996, the year following the development of our Vision Statement, we saw the largest increase in annual revenue at that point in the firm's history, with a 28 percent year-over-year increase. In the decade that followed, Kahler Slater's revenue rose 175 percent. Additionally, the enterprise has been ranked as one of the "50 Best Small and Medium Companies to Work for in America" for six years running (2004–2009) by the Great Place to Work® Institute, in conjunction with *HR Magazine*—one of only two small companies in the country to remain on the list every year since its inception. The design consultancy of Zweig White named us one of the top 10 architecture firms in the country in 2006 in their inaugural employment excellence program.

Other honors and awards have followed, but the one that means the most to us is our client retention rate. For the most recent 10 years, more than 90 percent of our work is repeat work from past client relationships. Some years, that number has been as high as 96 percent.

We believe our success is a result of understanding our own unique difference in the marketplace, and in clearly defining what we believe and why we exist, which drives how we behave and what we offer to our customers and staff. This has led to our own transformation, and has provided us with the experience and expertise to lead others down a similar path toward their own organizational transformations. It's a path that has been firmly established and well-trod through the years. We believe any organization that is brave enough to embark upon it, and dedicated enough to stay the course, will ultimately find itself transformed in a way that clearly and authentically differentiates it from its competition, and which it can continue to leverage for long-term success.

In working to achieve our own organizational transformation, we practiced what we preached, beginning by analyzing our own 4Ps: What *Perception* did Kahler Slater have in the marketplace, and how did we want our clients, staff, and the world at large to perceive us? How well did our *People* represent who we are and what we are about? What *Products and Services* did we produce or provide as an outcome of our processes? And how well did our *Place*—the physical environments in which we conduct business—support and make manifest our vision for the organization?

Thus was born our manifesto for total experience design. And we have been able to apply this philosophy successfully to our projects with clients in all our areas of specialization, from hospitals to hotels, to corporate offices and classrooms. It works well, embraces and encompasses the total customer and employee experience, and offers ample flexibility to adapt to additional specialties into which we may yet grow.

The simple notion that it might be a good idea to ask our people what they were passionate about has helped Kahler Slater grow into the holistic design enterprise that it is today. This passion provided the fuel that our own organization needed to confirm our collective vision. And it helped us create the model we've used to help other businesses and organizations define their own visions for the transformational environments and experiences they wish to design for their clients, their clients' clients, and their employees.

How One CEO became Three Executive Officers (3EOs)

As David Kahler was winding down his leadership at Kahler Slater, there were three of us who gradually took over many of his leadership duties: George Meyer, Jim Rasche and me. And each of us found that we liked many aspects of being a CEO (although not all of them), and we especially liked a combination of CEO duties with our "day jobs"—working with clients on projects. As David's retirement date got closer and closer, we three took on more and more responsibilities growing Kahler Slater into a national firm, with our eyes on a global presence before too long. If there could only be one CEO upon David's retirement, we three were going to have to have a difficult conversation very soon. Which one of us was going to become the new David? Which one of us wanted that role the most, and who had the best aptitude for taking on the entire CEO role, and not just cherry picking the parts we liked the best?

First we did some surveying and benchmarking. We started by talking with other CEOs, both in and out of our industry. Exactly what did they do? What were their skill sets? What did they like about their jobs? What didn't they like about their jobs? We discovered that for all of the people we interviewed, it was not unusual for CEOs to *not* be doing the work that made them successful CEOs in the first place. For the most part, those activities that made them stand out because of their passions and talents were gone. Instead they were caught up in day-to-day senior management issues and decisions, operations, finance, the running of the firm. Many of the people we spoke with longed for the days of working directly with clients on projects. We knew we would, too.

The next thing we did was put ourselves through rigorous personality inventory tests, as well as various strengths and weakness assessments. When we analyzed the information, we found that none of us had *all* the qualities and skill sets that would make up the perfect CEO. Through our research, we had come up with what we call the Nine Realms of the CEO, and we discovered that each of us covered three realms. Together, as a threesome, we covered all the bases in a very balanced way:

George: Fun, Quality, Finances
Jim: Vision, People, Creativity
Jill: Identity, Strategy, Relationships

So we said to each other, "If we're each covering a third of the CEO job, why don't we just share it?" David liked the idea. (He had already had a successful experience putting together a balanced leadership team at the Milwaukee Art Museum, pairing a finance director with an art director.)

Then we presented the idea to the staff, who (nonplused) said, "That's what you're doing already."

Our clients didn't get it as quickly, though. They wanted to know who, when push comes to shove, would be the ultimate *decider*. The answer remains the same: the three of us. In the nine years we have been working together this way, we've never called for a vote on any issue. We have arrived at decisions together. Because we have very obvious and distinctive skill sets, we'll challenge each other, even argue with one other at times. But we also defer to the person who owns the necessary skill, strength, or expertise required by the decision being made, because we trust each other to make the right decisions. Our Vision Statement remains the guide—if there is any doubt among the three of us as to which way to go, we simply revisit our vision, and the answer becomes obvious.

Even though it sometimes might take longer for a decision to be made, the actual execution of the decision more than makes up for any delay. The quality of that decision will stand the test of time, because with our varied skill sets and personalities, you can bet that we've approached the issue from every angle. Therefore, execution typically goes much faster and more smoothly.

But, if there isn't trust among the shared leadership team, forget about it. If you can't trust, and if you can't check your ego at the door, do not bother with this arrangement. For most companies in most industries, the pressure placed upon the CEO is challenging enough. But to try to be Super CEO and be all things to all people has got to be a nightmare. Here, the pressure's off. We know we're not perfect, but we also know where we can get support. Not only from each other, but also from the entire firm.

Our approach to executive leadership, as well as the entire way in which the firm is run, may not be for everyone—which is exactly the point of this book. Each organization needs to discover its own authentic organizational fingerprint, and make it manifest in the way that is the most real for them. It's a challenging task, but with the right framework, process, and attitude, it can be done.

NOTES

CHAPTER 1

1. Harry Torczyner, *Magritte: Ideas and Images* (New York: Harry N. Abrams, Inc, 1977), 71.

2. Tom McGehee, *Whoosh: Business in the Fast Lane* (New York: Basic Books, 2001), 176.

3. Sheila Bonini, David Court, and Alberto Marchi, "Rebuilding Corporate Reputations," June, 2009 McKinsey Quarterly, http://www.mckinseyquarterly.com/Rebuilding_corporate_reputations_2367.

4. Jack Trout, *Differentiate or Die: Survival in Our Era of Killer Competition* (New York: John Wiley & Sons, 2000), 21.

5. Ibid., 25.

6. Marc Gobe, *Emotional Branding: The New Paradigm for Connecting Brands to People* (New York: Allworth Press, 2001), xiv.

CHAPTER 2

1. B. Joseph Pine and James H. Gilmore, *The Experience Economy: Work Is Theatre and Every Business a Stage* (Boston: Harvard Business School Press, 1999), 103.

CHAPTER 3

1. "What Price Reputation?" *BusinessWeek*, July 9, 2007, http://www.businesseek.com/magazine/content/07_28/b4042050.htm.

2. B. Joseph Pine and James H. Gilmore, *The Experience Economy: Work Is Theatre and Every Business a Stage* (Boston: Harvard Business School Press, 1999), 60.

CHAPTER 4

1. Theresa Amabile and Mukti Khaire, "Creativity and the Role of the Leader," *Harvard Business Review* (October 2008).

2. Ed Catmull, "How Pixar Fosters Collective Creativity," *Harvard Business Review* (September 2008).

CHAPTER 6

1. Larry K. Michaealsen, Arletta Bauman Knight, and L. Dee Fink, *Team-based Learning: A Transformative Use of Small Groups in College Learning* (Sterling, VA: Stylus Publishing, 2004).

2. Wendy Feuer and Ralph Steinglass, FAIA, "Observations on Collaborations," American Institute of Architects Committee on Design Forum, 1999.

CHAPTER 9

1. Bruce W. Tuckman, "Developmental Sequence in Small Groups," *Psychological Bulletin* 63 (1965): 384–399.

EPILOGUE

1. Margery Williams, *The Velveteen Rabbit* (Deerfield Beach, FL: HCI, 2005), 17.

INDEX

Note: A page number followed by f means the reference is to a figure on the indicated page.

About the Author

Jill J. Morin is a co-chief executive for Kahler Slater, an interdisciplinary design, planning, and consulting firm. Morin is a popular speaker on total experience design, creativity, and creating a best place to work. Under her leadership, Kahler Slater has been named one of the Best Small and Medium Companies to Work For in America for the past six years by the Great Place to Work® Institute and the Society for Human Resource Management.

Founded in 1908, Kahler Slater works with clients throughout the world including Google, Monster.com, Manpower, Robert Redford's Sundance 608, Mayo Health System, University of Wisconsin, and the National University Hospital of Singapore to define and manifest their authentic Organizational Visions through the design of ideal total experiences.

Morin can be reached at jillmorin@bettermakeitreal.com.